Mathematics Practice for the 2023-2024 SHSAT Exam

10 Practice Tests with Detailed Answer Explanations

VIKTORIYA FURINA, MPA

ISBN: 9798846129078

DEDICATION

This book is dedicated to the many students who, throughout the years with their perseverance and ultimate success, have greatly impacted my life.

A special thank you to the wonderful math tutors who work at ExamIQ.

To Mikhael, Jonathan, and David

CONTENTS

SHSAT Mathematics Practice Test #1:

1. What is the positive value of x that makes the equation below true?

$$x^2 + 6x - 16 = 0$$

2. If triangle ABC is a right triangle, what is the value of x?

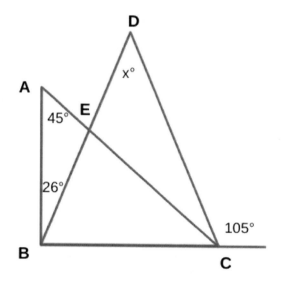

3. Turn the expression below to a decimal.

$$\frac{6}{16} + \frac{1}{2} + \frac{3}{4} + \frac{5}{8}$$

4. What is the area of a circle, if the diameter is 6 units? Round to the nearest tenth place.

5. 9x - 3y = 6

   6x + 3y = 24

   What is the value of x in the systems of equations above?

6. What is the value of the expression, $-3\frac{7}{10} \div 2\frac{1}{4}$?

    A) $\frac{-90}{148}$

    B) $\frac{-44}{93}$

    C) $\frac{-92}{47}$

    D) $\frac{-74}{45}$

7. Using the approximation 2.54 centimeters = 1 inch, how many centimeters are in 5 feet 8 inches?

    A) 26.77 centimeters

    B) 172.72 centimeters

    C) 101.60 centimeters

    D) 147.32 centimeters

8. What is the greatest prime factor of 117?

    A) 3

    B) 9

    C) 13

    D) 39

9. If p is a multiple of 3, which of the following must also be a multiple of 3?

    A) $2p + 2$

    B) $3p + 4$

    C) $5p + 9$

    D) $6p + 10$

10. Daria rents a bicycle for a flat fee of $50. After the first 15 miles, she must pay $0.35 per mile. If she pays $60.50 in total, how many miles did Daria travel on her bicycle?

    A) 30 miles

    B) 45 miles

    C) 60 miles

    D) 75 miles

11. What is the value of x in the equation, $\frac{x-8}{6} + \frac{4}{3} = 1$?

    A) x = 6

    B) x = 7

    C) x = 8

    D) x = 9

12. If a cylinder has a height of 6 feet and the base has an area of 36π square inches, what is the volume of the cylinder? Use $\pi = 3.14$.

    A) 56.52 cubic feet

    B) 4.71 cubic feet

    C) 244.92 cubic feet

    D) 678.24 cubic feet

13. A stack of cards has 6 green cards. The probability of choosing a green card from the stack is $\frac{3}{8}$. How many of the cards in the stack are not green?

    A) 10 cards

    B) 12 cards

    C) 16 cards

    D) 18 cards

14. What is the simplest form of $\frac{686}{1862}$?

    A) $\frac{1}{3}$

    B) $\frac{7}{17}$

    C) $\frac{7}{19}$

    D) $\frac{2}{5}$

15. What is a possible value of x in the inequality below?

$$60x + 20 \leq 320$$

    A) 8

    B) 7

    C) 6

    D) 5

16. If -14y + 10x = 17, what is x in terms of y?

    A) $x = 17 - \frac{7}{5}y$

    B) $x = \frac{17}{10} - \frac{7}{5}y$

    C) $x = \frac{17}{10} + \frac{7}{5}y$

    D) $x = 17 + \frac{7}{5}y$

17. An unmarked, perfectly straight stick will be placed end over end to measure a distance of exactly 72 feet. The same stick will be used in the same way to measure a distance of exactly 30 feet. What is the length of the longest possible stick that can be used for both measurements?

    A) 3 ft.

    B) 4 ft.

    C) 6 ft.

    D) 8 ft.

18. Solve for x: $|-3(4x + 2)| \leq 30$

    A) $-3 \geq x \leq 2$

    B) $-3 \leq x \leq 2$

    C) $-3 \geq x \geq 2$

    D) $-3 \leq x \geq 2$

19. The sum of two consecutive integers is 23. If 3 is added to the smaller number, and 5 is subtracted from the larger number, what is the product of the two numbers?

    A) 90

    B) 93

    C) 98

    D) 121

20. If angle ABC = $3x + 4°$, angle BAC = $4x - 4°$, and angle BCD = $6x + 20°$, what is the measurement of angle BCA?

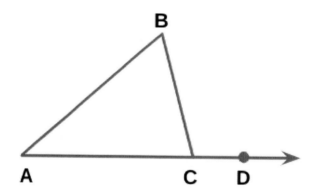

    A) 40°

    B) 140°

    C) 50°

    D) 130°

21. $\frac{9-4x}{3} = 11$

What is the value of x in the expression above?

    A) -5

    B) -6

    C) -7

    D) -8

22. $8\sqrt{6} - 4\sqrt{48} =$

    A) $16\sqrt{3} - 4\sqrt{3}$

    B) $8\sqrt{6} - 16\sqrt{3}$

    C) $8\sqrt{6} - 16\sqrt{6}$

    D) $8\sqrt{6} - 12\sqrt{4}$

23. $\frac{3}{5}$ of the students in an auditorium are boys. About $\frac{1}{3}$ of the girls are in the 6th grade. If there are 600 students in the auditorium, how many of them are 6th grade girls?

    A) 150 students

    B) 120 students

    C) 90 students

    D) 80 students

24. $\left|\frac{4x^2}{5}\right| = 20$

In the equation above, what is the value of x?

    A) -5

    B) 6

    C) -4

    D) 0.5

25. Betty is running at a rate of 4 meters per second. At this same rate, how long will it take for her to finish a 5-kilometer race? Round to the nearest hundredth of a minute.

    A) 8.45 minutes

    B) 16.29 minutes

    C) 20.83 minutes

    D) 37.80 minutes

26. What is the greatest common factor of 91 and 98?

    A) 2

    B) 7

    C) 13

    D) 14

27. A hole in the shape of a rectangular prism is being dug at a construction site. The width of the hole is 5 feet, and the length of the hole is 12 feet. If 180 cubic feet of cement is used to completely fill in the hole, how deep was the hole?

    A) 2 feet

    B) 3 feet

    C) 4 feet

    D) 5 feet

28. Angles A and B are supplementary angles. If angle A is 15 degrees less than half of angle B, what is the value of angle A?

    A) 50

    B) 55

    C) 60

    D) 65

29. In a box of chocolate, there are 80 chocolates: 25 of them are dark chocolate, 44 of them are white chocolate, and the rest are milk chocolate. What is the probability of NOT getting dark chocolate?

   A) $\frac{5}{16}$

   B) $\frac{11}{16}$

   C) $\frac{1}{2}$

   D) $\frac{11}{80}$

30. If $5^x = \sqrt{625}$, then x =

   A) 0.5

   B) 1

   C) 2

   D) 3

31.

Color	Number of people
Blue	37
Red	11
Green	24
Black	28

People were asked what their favorite color is. How much greater is the percentage of people who like blue and black than the percentage of people who like green and red?

A) $\frac{2}{100}$

B) $\frac{49}{100}$

C) $\frac{30}{100}$

D) $\frac{24}{100}$

32. If $s = \frac{t}{g}$ and $x = \frac{p}{r}$, what is $\frac{x}{s}$ equal to?

A. $\frac{pg}{rt}$

B. $\frac{pt}{rg}$

C. $\frac{rt}{pg}$

D. $\frac{rg}{pt}$

EXAMIQ

33. A cake is in the shape of a cylinder. It is 4 inches tall with a radius of 6 inches. If the cake is cut into 8 equal slices, what is the volume of one slice? Use π=3.14.

    A) 75.36 cubic inches

    B) 6.34 cubic inches

    C) 7.23 cubic inches

    D) 56.52 cubic inches

34. A farmer measures the height of her trees. She finds that the tallest tree in her farm is 31 feet tall, and the smallest tree is 24 feet tall. Which inequality describes the range of heights of her trees?

    A) $24 < x < 31$

    B) $24 \geq x \geq 31$

    C) $24 \leq x \leq 31$

    D) $24 \leq x \geq 31$

35. If, $\frac{6}{5x-5} = \frac{3}{5}$

    In the equation above, what is the value of x?

    A) 5

    B) 3

    C) $\frac{3}{5}$

    D) 2

36. Marie makes x number of cookies. Sharon makes 4 fewer than 3 times the number of cookies Marie makes. If Benson makes half as many as the number of cookies Sharon makes, how many cookies did Benson make, in terms of x ?

    A) 3x-4

    B) $2x - \frac{3}{2}$

    C) x+4

    D) $-2 + \frac{3x}{2}$

37. $2\frac{1}{2} + 5\frac{3}{4} + 1\frac{7}{8}$

What is the value of the expression shown above?

A) $\frac{128}{16}$

B) $\frac{146}{16}$

C) $\frac{158}{16}$

D) $\frac{162}{16}$

38. 252 people want to get over a river. Sailboats carry 45 people each, and tugboats carry 12 people each. If only 10 boats are used, how many sailboats and tugboats are needed to get everyone across?

A) 2 sailboats and 3 tugboats

B) 3 sailboats and 7 tugboats

C) 4 sailboats and 6 tugboats

D) 5 sailboats and 5 tugboats

39. What is the slope of the line that is parallel to the line that goes through the points A(3,-1) and B(-3,-3)?

A) $\frac{1}{3}$

B) 3

C) $\frac{3}{4}$

D) $1\frac{1}{3}$

40. There are 63 students in a gym class. How many teams of 16 students can be made?

A) 3

B) 4

C) 5

D) 6

41. Maria is reading a book with 216 pages. It took her 30 minutes to read 6 pages. At the same rate, how much time in TOTAL will it take her to finish reading?

   A) 8 hours

   B) 10 hours

   C) 14 hours

   D) 18 hours

42. What is the value of h in the equation, $3h^3 - 6 = 186$?

   A) 3

   B) 4

   C) 5

   D) 6

43. At 11 A.M, the temperature is 66°F. Throughout the day, the temperature increases by 2°F every hour. What will the temperature be by 6 P.M. in Celsius? Use $(F - 32) \times \frac{5}{9} = C$.

   A) 50°C

   B) 80 °C

   C) 26.7 °C

   D) 41.4 °C

44. What is the value of x in $\frac{2x+6}{3} = \frac{x+8}{2}$?

   A) x = 6

   B) x = 10

   C) x = 4

   D) x = 12

45. Given $\sqrt{4x} = 8$, what is x equal to?

    A) x = 16

    B) x = 7

    C) x = 4

    D) x = 2

46. What value of y makes the proportion below true?

$$8:y = 136:68$$

    A) 3

    B) 4

    C) 5

    D) 6

47. What is the mean of 24, 45, 3, and 28?

    A) 24

    B) 25

    C) 26

    D) 27

48. Brent and Larry are working on a group test together. Brent can solve 5 questions in 6 minutes. Larry can solve 10 questions in 10 minutes. What is the total number of questions both of them can complete in one hour?

    A) 80 questions

    B) 90 questions

    C) 100 questions

    D) 110 questions

49. What is the value of x in terms of y?

$$(4x - 3) - (2 + 3x) - 5 = y$$

    A) $x = y + 10$

    B) $x + 2 = y$

    C) $x = y$

    D) $x - 7 = y$

50. How many seconds are there in 4 hours and 20 minutes?

    A) 14,400

    B) 14,800

    C) 15,600

    D) 16,200

51. If 4 times the number minus 2 is equal to 5 times the number plus 12. What is the value of a number?

    A) - 14

    B) 14

    C) 12

    D) -12

52. What is the value of the expression below as an improper fraction?

$$8.625 - 3.75$$

    A) $\frac{36}{8}$

    B) $\frac{37}{8}$

    C) $\frac{38}{8}$

    D) $\frac{39}{8}$

53. The statement 40 added to the product of 7 and y exceeds 250. Which of the following represents the statement?

    A) $7y + 40 > 250$

    B) $7y + 40 < 250$

    C) $40 - 7y < 250$

    D) $40 - 7y > 250$

54. Which expression is equivalent to $\left(14^{\frac{5}{7}}\right)^{-2}$?

    A) $\frac{1}{14} \times \frac{1}{14^{\frac{10}{7}}}$

    B) $\frac{1}{14} \times \frac{1}{14^{\frac{3}{7}}}$

    C) $14 \times \frac{1}{14^{\frac{3}{7}}}$

    D) $-14 \times \frac{1}{14^{\frac{3}{7}}}$

55. The distance from Point A to Point B is 1,560 miles. A train travels the first 180 miles in 6 hours. If the train travels at that same rate, how much **longer** will it take to reach Point B? Round to the nearest hundredth place if necessary.

    A) 10.50 hours

    B) 26.54 hours

    C) 35.89 hours

    D) 46.00 hours

SHSAT Mathematics Practice Test #2:

1. A United States presidential coin is made from an alloy of four metals—copper, zinc, manganese, and nickel—with masses in the ratio of 177:12:7:4, respectively. The coin weighs a total of 8 grams. What is the mass of the zinc in this coin?

2. What is the value of x in $x^3 + 7^2 = 19 * 2^2$?

3. In the word "SMILE", there are 5 letters. How many different ways can the letters be arranged?

4. A diesel train left Miami and traveled toward the outermost station at an average speed of 25km/h. Sometime later, a freight train left in the same direction, but at an average speed of 40km/h. Having traveled for 10 hours, the freight train caught up with the diesel train. Find the number of hours the diesel train traveled before the freight train caught up with it.

5. If one of the faces of a square pyramid looks like the triangle below, what is the surface area of the square pyramid?

4 yards

6 yards

6. In a scale diagram, 0.6 centimeters represent 10 meters. How many centimeters represent 80 meters?

    A) 8.6 centimeters

    B) 1.4 centimeters

    C) 4.8 centimeters

    D) 8 centimeters

7. Find x. If x and y are complementary angles, and x is ¼ of y.

    A) 15°

    B) 18°

    C) 36°

    D) 72°

8. Which of the following numbers have factors that include the smallest factor (other than 1) of 91?

    A) 30

    B) 35

    C) 39

    D) 44

9. If $a^3 + \frac{9}{4} = 3b^2$, what is b in terms of a?

    A) $a = b^2 - \frac{3}{4}$

    B) $a = 3\sqrt[3]{b^2 - a}$

    C) $a = \sqrt[3]{b^2 - \frac{9}{a}}$

    D) $a = \sqrt[3]{3b^2 - \frac{9}{4}}$

10. A pyramid's base is a square. If one of the base's sides is 4 feet, and the height is 10 feet, approximately what is the volume of the pyramid in cubic feet?

    A) 13 cubic feet

    B) 36 cubic feet

    C) 53 cubic feet

    D) 64 cubic feet

11. There are 50 coins in a piggy bank that equal $10.25. If there are only dimes and quarters in the piggy bank, how many dimes are there in the piggybank?

    A) 5

    B) 15

    C) 20

    D) 25

12. 7 people are competing for 1st, 2nd, and 3rd place in a race. How many unique arrangements are there for the 3 positions?

    A) 21

    B) 343

    C) 210

    D) 5040

13. Mei is writing a paper for school. If she wrote 3 pages in 5 hours, how much **longer** will it take her to write a total of 8 pages?

    A) $8\frac{1}{3}$ hours

    B) $13\frac{1}{3}$ hours

    C) $5\frac{2}{3}$ hours

    D) $9\frac{2}{3}$ hours

14. (2x+6) - (3x-4) =

    A) -x+10

    B) x-2

    C) -x-2

    D) x+10

15. Which of the following is equal to 50% of $\frac{15}{10}$?

    A) 0.15

    B) 1.05

    C) 0.75

    D) 1.50

16. Mark has $100 in his wallet and earns $15 an hour. He wants to purchase a new game and console, which cost $470 in total. Which of the following algebraic inequalities show how many hours he needs to work?

    A) 15 + 100x < 470

    B) 15 + 100x > 470

    C) 15x + 100 < 470

    D) 15x + 100 > 470

17. How many positive even factors of 180 are greater than 10 and less than 60?

    A) 3

    B) 4

    C) 5

    D) 6

18.

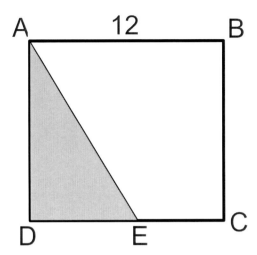

ABCD is a square. If E is the midpoint of DC what is the area of the shaded region?

A) 72

B) 36

C) 12

D) 6

19. What is the value of the expression: $\frac{2}{3}(\frac{9}{5}/\frac{9}{13}) + \frac{1}{2}$?

A) $\frac{7}{9}$

B) $\frac{23}{15}$

C) $\frac{3}{2}$

D) $\frac{67}{30}$

20. The set of possible values for *a* are {4,6,8,9,11}. What is the set of possible values of *b* if b = 3a + 1?

    A) {13,25,28}

    B) {13,19,25,28,34}

    C) {12,24,27}

    D) {12,18,24,27,33}

21. If Geri can run 6 miles per hour, what is her rate in feet per second?

    A) 5.6 feet per second

    B) 7.4 feet per second

    C) 8.8 feet per second

    D) 10.2 feet per second

22. What can x equal to in order to make the proportion below true?

    $$16:28 = x:42$$

    A) 24

    B) 28

    C) 32

    D) 38

23. If John gave Larry $5, Larry would have triple the amount of Steven's money. Which of the following expresses Larry's money (before being given $5) in terms of *x*, with *x* representing Steven's money?

    A) $3x$

    B) $3x - 5$

    C) $3x + 5$

    D) $3x - 15$

24. What is 20% of 15% of 30?

    A) 10.5

    B) 9.0

    C) 1.3

    D) 0.9

25. The surface area of a sphere is 200.96 cubic inches. What is the radius of the sphere? Use $\pi=3.14$.

    A) 2 inches

    B) 3 inches

    C) 4 inches

    D) 5 inches

26. Which of the following graphs describe the following inequality?

$$|-(x-3)| < 2$$

A)

B)

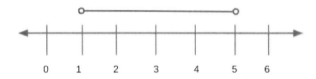

C)

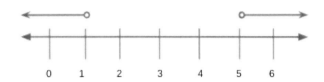

D)

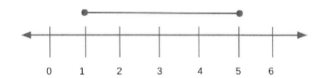

27. Matt scored a 76 on his first test, a 94 on his second test, and an 88 on his third test. What score does Matt need to score on his final, fourth, test in order to ensure an average of 86?

A) 82

B) 84

C) 86

D) 88

28. What is the value of y in the system of equations below?

$$8x + 4y = 92$$

$$x + 2y = 22$$

 A) 4
 B) 5
 C) 6
 D) 7

29. Dillian spends x dollars on clothing. Matty spends y dollars on clothing. The product of 2 less than three times the amount Dillian spent and 5 more than half the amount Matty spent, is equal to the amount of money Gordon spends on clothing. How much did Gordon spend in terms of x and y?

 A) $3xy - 3x + 4y + 4$
 B) $\frac{2}{3}xy - 6x + 3y + 5$
 C) $\frac{3}{2}xy + 15x - y - 10$
 D) $xy + 3x - 2y + 12$

30. What is the value of n in the equation below when expressed as a fraction?

n = 0.75 + 0.375

 A) $\frac{9}{4}$
 B) $\frac{9}{8}$
 C) $\frac{4}{9}$
 D) $\frac{8}{9}$

31. Chris is c years old now. Tim is 5 years older than Chris. Which of the following expressions represent Tim's age 5 years from now, in terms of c?

    A) c + 10
    B) c + 5
    C) c - 5
    D) c - 10

32. What is the value of x in terms of y and z in the equation below?
$$z(32 - 8x) = 4y$$

    A) $x = 3y - \frac{1}{2z}$
    B) $\frac{y}{3z} + 2 = x$
    C) $x = 4 - \frac{y}{2z}$
    D) $-\frac{z}{y} + 1 = x$

33. What is the least common multiple of 12, 15, and 21?

    A) 210
    B) 420
    C) 75
    D) 105

34. Between which two consecutive integers is $\frac{35}{6}$ located?

    A) 2 and 3
    B) 4 and 5
    C) 5 and 6
    D) 6 and 7

35. The probability of choosing a blue pen in a pencil box is $\frac{1}{8}$, which of the following could be the number of total pens in the box?

    A) 14

    B) 22

    C) 27

    D) 32

36. What is the value of n in $3(9 + 4) = n^2 + 3$?

    A) n = 2

    B) n = 5

    C) n = 6

    D) n = 9

37. Ms. Smith has 30 students per class, she teaches 4 classes. She reported to the principal that only 70% of all her students will pass the class this year. How many students will pass this year?

    A) 25

    B) 82

    C) 84

    D) 21

38. An elm tree and an oak tree are both the same height. The elm tree grows at a rate of 5 inches per week. The oak tree grows at a rate of 0.75 inches per day. How much taller is the oak tree than the elm tree after two months? Assume there are 4 weeks in each month.

    A) They are still the same height.

    B) 1 inch

    C) 2 inches

    D) 3 inches

39.   If the triangle below is an isosceles triangle, what is the measure of angle A?

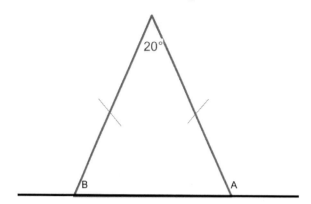

    A) 80°

    B) 100°

    C) 110°

    D) 120°

40. It takes Vanessa 1.75 hours to finish a 40-question test. It takes Kelly 3.00 hours to take that same test. How much faster does it take Vanessa to complete a question than Kelly, in seconds?

    A) 106.2 seconds

    B) 112.5 seconds

    C) 130.4 seconds

    D) 142.5 seconds

41. $4(y - 7) + 8(1 - 6y) = 24$. What does y equal?

    A) $y = 4$

    B) $y = -8$

    C) $y = -1$

    D) $y = 9$

42. In a foreign country, the currency conversion rate is 1 coin = 0.25 bill. How many coins are equal to 15 bills?

    A) 35

    B) 40

    C) 55

    D) 60

43. What is the value of the expression $\frac{5}{3} + \frac{10}{3} * 1\frac{7}{15}$?

    A) $\frac{59}{9}$

    B) $\frac{41}{29}$

    C) $\frac{73}{18}$

    D) $\frac{37}{15}$

44. $10(n + 2) = 8n$

    What is the value of n in the equation above?

    A) $n = 24$

    B) $n = -4$

    C) $n = 8$

    D) $n = -10$

45. What is the value of x in terms of y and z?

$$6x - y = 3z$$

    A) $\frac{z}{2} + \frac{y}{6} = x$

    B) $x = \frac{z+3y}{6}$

    C) $\frac{2}{y} - \frac{z}{6} = x$

    D) $x = \frac{6+3y}{z}$

46. One of the faces on a cube has an area of 5 units squared. What is the volume of the cube?

    A) $2\sqrt{5}\ units^3$

    B) $15\ units^3$

    C) $5\sqrt{5}\ units^3$

    D) $25\ units^3$

47. A recipe for soup asks for 3 cups of carrots for every 8 cups of tomatoes. If Charlie uses 56 cups of tomatoes, how many carrots should he use if he wants to follow the recipe?

    A) 12 cups

    B) 15 cups

    C) 18 cups

    D) 21 cups

48. Which of the following is the largest prime number that is 3 more than a positive multiple of 5?

    A) 18

    B) 23

    C) 28

    D) 43

49. What is the mode of the set: 51,77,34,99,44,77,88,34,77?

    A) 44

    B) 34

    C) 51

    D) 77

50. The area of the parallelogram is 220 square inches. Line AB = 2(x-3) and line BC = x+2. What is the value of x?

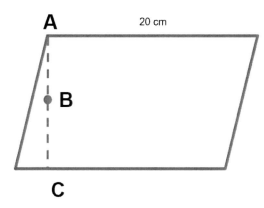

A) 5

B) 6

C) 7

D) 8

51. $4\frac{2}{3}+\frac{1}{10}\times\frac{1}{6}=$

A) $\frac{180}{15}$

B) 1

C) $\frac{15}{14}$

D) $\frac{281}{60}$

52. $7x + 2y = -19$

$-x + 2y = 21$

What is the intersection point between the two equations above?

A) $(2,-7)$

B) $(-4,-6)$

C) $(5,-7)$

D) $(-5,8)$

53. Jake has 20 markers in a bag: 6 green markers, 9 blue markers, and 5 red markers. If he adds 3 green markers and draws a marker at random, what is the probability that he chooses a blue marker?

    A) $\frac{5}{23}$

    B) $\frac{6}{23}$

    C) $\frac{9}{23}$

    D) $\frac{15}{23}$

54. Solve for x:

    $\frac{5x+9}{3} = 19$

    A) 6.8

    B) 7.0

    C) 8.2

    D) 9.6

55. The surface area of a sphere is 314 cubic meters. What is the diameter of the sphere? Use π=3.14.

    A) 5 meters

    B) 10 meters

    C) 6 meters

    D) 12 meters

SHSAT Mathematics Practice Test #3:

1. How many multiples of 6 are between 20 and 80?

2. Janice and Will go to a furniture store. Will pays $300 for a table and 6 chairs. Janice buys twice the number of tables as Will and half as many chairs as Will. She needs to pay $375. What is the cost of one chair?

3. What is the value of B?

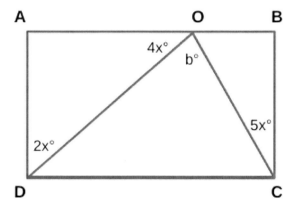

4. A song plays on the radio every 15 minutes. Assuming the radio show continues for the entire day, how many times a day does the song play?

5. Jason is a waiter at a restaurant. If he receives $20 in tips per hour, what is the least number of hours he has to work if he wants to buy $310 shoes?

6. The distance between Sam's home and his school is 3,168 feet. If Sam walks at a rate of 4.4 feet per second, how long will it take for Sam to walk home from school?

    A) 9 minutes

    B) 10 minutes

    C) 11 minutes

    D) 12 minutes

7. In a school, the ratio between boys to girls is 3 to 4. There are 300 more girls than boys. How many students are in this school?

    A) 2100

    B) 525

    C) 1200

    D) 900

8. What is the least common multiple of 6, 9, and 48?

    A) 24

    B) 48

    C) 72

    D) 144

9. Find the value of x if $3^x = 27^2$.

    A) 2

    B) 3

    C) 5

    D) 6

10. What is the greatest possible value of the inequality below?

$$5x + 1 < 3x + 17$$

   A) 5
   B) 6
   C) 7
   D) 8

11. At a store, customers can buy a pack of 3 batteries for the price of $5.40, or they can buy a pack of 15 batteries for $18.00. What is the difference between the unit price of the two battery packs?

   A) $0.60
   B) $0.75
   C) $0.89
   D) They are the same price.

12. A circle is inscribed inside of a square. If the circumference of the circle is 8π inches, what is the perimeter of the square?

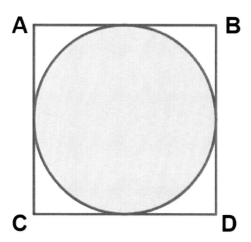

   A) 16 inches
   B) 32 inches
   C) 64 inches
   D) 216 inches

13. A candy store has a jar of gumballs: 3 pink, 5 green, 7 yellow, 11 blue, and 12 red. If one ball is picked at random from the jar, what is the probability the gumball will be red?

   A) $\frac{1}{29}$

   B) $\frac{4}{19}$

   C) $\frac{3}{8}$

   D) $\frac{6}{19}$

14. In a set of consecutive integers from 30 to 70, how many integers are multiples of 4?

   A) 7

   B) 8

   C) 9

   D) 10

15. Simplify this expression:

   $4(7 + 8x) - (22 - 3x)$

   A) 35x+6

   B) 29x+6

   C) 35x+50

   D) 29x+50

16. In the isosceles triangle ABC, line segments AB and BC are equal in length. Angle B is equal to 30 degrees. What is the measure of angle A?

   A) 60

   B) 65

   C) 70

   D) 75

17. If 5x+2y= 15, what is x in terms of y?

    A) $x = -\frac{2}{5}y+15$

    B) $x = \frac{2}{5}y+15$

    C) $x = -\frac{2}{5}y+3$

    D) $x = \frac{2}{5}y+3$

18. Which of the following numbers can be divided by 7?

    A) 99

    B) 104

    C) 119

    D) 125

19. A rectangular prism has a height of 4 cm. The length is half as much as the height, and the width is three times as large as the length. What is the volume of the rectangular prism?

    A) 10 cubic centimeters

    B) 21 cubic centimeters

    C) 36 cubic centimeters

    D) 48 cubic centimeters

20. What is 20% of 45% of 700?

    A) 63

    B) 77

    C) 252

    D) 308

21. In a scale diagram, 0.6 centimeters represent 10 meters. How many centimeters represent 80 meters?

    A) 8.6 centimeters

    B) 1.4 centimeters

    C) 4.8 centimeters

    D) 8 centimeters

22. What is n equal to if $5n^3 - 323 = -\sqrt[3]{27}$?

    A) n = 1

    B) n = 3

    C) n = 4

    D) n = 9

23. How many positive, even factors of 48 are greater than 24 and less than 48?

    A) 0

    B) 1

    C) 2

    D) 12

24. If $\frac{a}{b} = 7$ and $a + 9 = 23$, what is the value of $4a + 3b$?

    A) 32

    B) 48

    C) 62

    D) 15

25. What is the volume of a globe that is 6 inches tall? Use π=3.14. Round to the nearest hundredth place if necessary. Use the volume formula of a sphere, $\frac{4}{3}\pi r^3$.

    A) 25.12 cubic inches

    B) 113.04 cubic inches

    C) 904.32 cubic inches

    D) 7234.56 cubic inches

26. Ted is mowing his lawn. If it takes Ted 3 hours to mow a 2,775-yard lawn, how long will it take him to mow a 4,856.25-yard lawn?

    A) 4 hours and 25 minutes

    B) 4 hours and 15 minutes

    C) 5 hours and 25 minutes

    D) 5 hours and 15 minutes

27. $5x + 4y = -7$

    $-5x - 2y = 1$

    What is the value of x in the system of equations above?

    A) $x = 2$

    B) $x = -3$

    C) $x = 1$

    D) $x = 5$

28. What is four times 30% of 260?

    A) 312

    B) 544

    C) 682

    D) 728

29. If $x^2 + 4 = 53$, what is the value of x?

    A) x = 7

    B) x = 4

    C) x = 8

    D) x = 2

30. Which inequality represents the numbers you can roll on a dice?

    A) $1 < x < 6$

    B) $1 \leq x \leq 6$

    C) $1 < x > 6$

    D) $1 < x \geq 6$

31. If $-7a + 8b = 42$, what is a in terms of b?

    A) $a = 6 - \dfrac{8b}{7}$

    B) $a = -5 - \dfrac{7b}{8}$

    C) $a = -6 + \dfrac{8b}{7}$

    D) $a = -5 + \dfrac{7b}{78}$

32. Two cards are drawn from a deck of 52 cards. Assuming the cards are put back into the deck after they are drawn, what is the probability that one card is a heart and one is a diamond?

    A) $\dfrac{1}{13}$

    B) $\dfrac{1}{52}$

    C) $\dfrac{1}{16}$

    D) $\dfrac{1}{139}$

33.

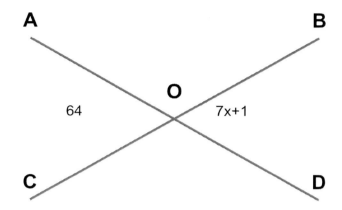

In the diagram above, what is the value of x?

A) 8

B) 9

C) 10

D) 11

34. What is the value of 25% of the expression $\frac{17}{14} * \frac{22}{3}$?

A) $\frac{187}{84}$

B) $\frac{187}{21}$

C) $\frac{179}{49}$

D) $\frac{179}{196}$

35. The sum of two consecutive, odd integers is 168. Which integer is the greater number?

A) 81

B) 83

C) 85

D) 87

36. If there is a ratio of 3:4 boys to girls on a 21-person sports team, what is the number of girls on the team?

    A) 9 girls

    B) 10 girls

    C) 12 girls

    D) 13 girls

37. What is the value of a in terms of b?

$$(18a - 12) - (-3a + 9) = 3b$$

    A) $a = \frac{b}{7} + 1$

    B) $a = \frac{4b}{3}$

    C) $a = \frac{5}{b}$

    D) $a = b + 7$

38. What number is the ones digit of 7^7?

    A) 1

    B) 7

    C) 9

    D) 3

39. What is the surface area of a cube with a side length of 8?

    A) 256

    B) 288

    C) 384

    D) 512

40. For what value of x is $\frac{3}{16} = \frac{2x}{8}$?

    A) $x = \frac{1}{4}$

    B) $x = \frac{3}{4}$

    C) $x = 2$

    D) $x = \frac{4}{3}$

41. What is the least possible value of $3x^2 - 15$ if $x \geq 5$?

    A) 50

    B) 60

    C) 70

    D) 80

42. There are 56 seniors, 48 juniors, 64 sophomores, and 70 freshmen in a high school. What is the proportion between the number of freshmen to the total student population?

    A) 1:3

    B) 11:29

    C) 5:17

    D) 13:43

43. If $2(\frac{3}{8} - \frac{1}{4})^2 x = \frac{1}{2}$, what is the value of x?

    A) 14

    B) 16

    C) 18

    D) 20

44. What is the value of x in $2^x - 5 = 2(3 + 2) + 1$?

    A) x = 7

    B) x = 4

    C) x = 5

    D) x = 2

45. The ratio of boys to girls in a science class is 3:8. The total number of kids in the science class is 88. How many girls are in the science class?

    A) 3

    B) 8

    C) 24

    D) 64

46. What is the greatest prime factor of 498?

    A) 13

    B) 5

    C) 83

    D) 53

47. To rent a bike, you can either to pay a flat fee of $30 and pay $3 every mile you bike, OR you can just pay $5 for each mile biked. Assume x is the number of miles biked and y is the total amount of money paid. Choose a system of equations to describe this situation.

    A) $x = 30 + 3y$

       $5x = y$

    B) $30 + 5x = y$

       $3x = y$

    C) $3x + 5x = y$

       $30 = y$

    D) $x = \frac{y-30}{3}$

       $5x = y$

48. $\frac{x-2x}{2x} = -\frac{1}{2}$. What is the value of x?

    A) $x = 0$

    B) $x = 1$

    C) All real numbers

    D) No answers

49. A cube has a volume of 216 cubic inches. What is the area of one of its faces?

    A) 25 square inches

    B) 36 square inches

    C) 49 square inches

    D) 64 square inches

50. What is the value of y in $\sqrt{18y} = 2^2 - 1$?

    A) $y = 2$

    B) $y = 4$

    C) $y = \dfrac{1}{3}$

    D) $y = \dfrac{1}{2}$

51. Gabriella left Alexa's house and traveled toward a lake at an average speed of 25mph. Some time later, Tina left Alexa's house traveling in the exact opposite direction with an average speed of 35mph. After Tina had traveled for 2 hours, she and Gabriella were 120mi apart. How long did Gabriella travel?

    A) 4 hours

    B) 5 hours

    C) 1 hour

    D) 2 hours

52. As a waiter, Timothy earns \$20/hour. He gets a 15% raise. What is the difference between his new salary in 5 hours compared to his old salary in 5 hours?

    A) \$10

    B) \$15

    C) \$20

    D) \$25

53. Which of the following numbers is greater than ⅕?

    A) $\dfrac{1}{6}$

    B) $\dfrac{2}{11}$

    C) 0.23

    D) $\dfrac{202}{1054}$

54. When $-8x - 9y = 17$, what is y in terms of x?

    A) $\frac{17+8x}{9}$

    B) $\frac{17-8x}{9}$

    C) $-\frac{17+8x}{9}$

    D) $-\frac{17-8x}{9}$

55. If 3 feet = 6^x inches, what is the value of x?

    A) 1

    B) 2

    C) 3

    D) 4

SHSAT Mathematics Practice Test #4:

1. What is the second number of three consecutive numbers' products if the product is equal to 210?

2. A cylinder with a height of 10 inches and a radius of 5 inches is 30% filled with water. How much of the cylinder is filled with water? Use $\pi = 3.14$. Round to the nearest cubic inch.

3. Assume line $\underline{AB}$ is parallel to lines $\underline{CD}$ and $\underline{EF}$. If line $\underline{AE}$ is parallel to line $\underline{BF}$, what is 2x-y?

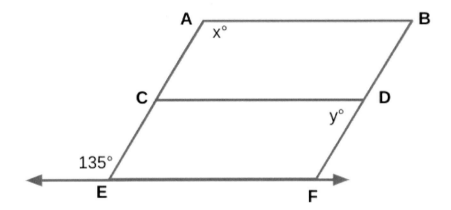

4. What is the value of x in $3(4 + x) = 9(x - 2)$?

5. In a school, there are 4,200 students. 40% of them are female and 25% of the females' favorite subject is math. How many female students' favorite subject is math?

6. What is the value of x in $8x + 3(12 + x) = -8$?

    A) x = -4

    B) x = -8

    C) x = 3

    D) x = 6

7. A passenger train left a city and traveled towards a repair station at a speed of 56km/h. A cattle train left three hours later and traveled towards the same station with a speed of 80 km/h. How many hours did the passenger train travel before the cattle train caught up?

    A) 10 hours

    B) 16 hours

    C) 4 hours

    D) 15 hours

8. A side of a cube is equal to $4x^3$. What is the surface area of the cube?

    A) $24x^3$

    B) $64x^6$

    C) $78x^6$

    D) $96x^6$

9. What is the least common multiple of 3, 8, and 14?

    A) 48

    B) 96

    C) 168

    D) 140

10. If a 3-meter tall tree grew by 64 centimeters, by what percentage did it grow? Round to the nearest hundredth place.

    A) 10.66%

    B) 15.00%

    C) 18.56%

    D) 21.33%

11. The test scores of a class were recorded on the table below:

Students	Scores
Johnny	92
Christy	77
Manny	82
Simon	100
Ethan	88
David	100

What is the difference between David's score and the median score?

    A) 2

    B) 8

    C) 10

    D) 22

12. What is the value of x in the equation, $\frac{x-7}{6} = -\frac{11}{4}$?

    A) $x = -4.3$

    B) $x = -9.5$

    C) $x = -11.6$

    D) $x = -11.0$

13. If n is an odd number, which of the following is an odd number?

    A) 2n

    B) 3n

    C) 4n

    D) 6n

14. What is 250% of 150?

    A) 225

    B) 375

    C) 400

    D) 525

15. What is half the value of a?

$$\frac{1}{8}a + \frac{3}{4}b = 34$$

    A) $173 - 4b$

    B) $272 - 6b$

    C) $346 - 8b$

    D) $136 - 3b$

16. What is the value of n in $5n - 7 = n - 1$?

    A) n = 10

    B) n = $\frac{2}{6}$

    C) n = 3

    D) n = $\frac{3}{2}$

17. The reciprocal of $\frac{1}{6}$ is added to the reciprocal of 4. What is the reciprocal of their sum?

    A) $\frac{25}{4}$

    B) $\frac{9}{16}$

    C) $\frac{4}{25}$

    D) $\frac{1}{4}$

18. The perimeter of a rectangle is 154 inches. If the ratio between the two sides is 5:2, what is the length and width of the rectangle?

    A) 45 in by 18 in

    B) 50 in by 20 in

    C) 55 in by 22 in

    D) 60 in by 24 in

19. What is the solution to the system of equations below?

$$2y + 20 = 10$$
$$5x + 4y = 20$$

    A) $(0, -5)$

    B) $(-4, 7)$

    C) $(8, -5)$

    D) $(5, -7)$

20. The decimal *0.06* can be written as the fraction $\frac{x}{50}$. What is the value of x ?

    A) 3

    B) 6

    C) 12

    D) 30

21. Charles bought $120 worth of groceries. After using a rewards card, 15% was taken off of his total. If a sales tax of 9% was applied, what was the total cost?

    A) $110.56

    B) $111.18

    C) $115.57

    D) $116.92

22. The sum of the numbers a, b, and c is 95. The ratio of a to b is 3:7, and the ratio of b to c is 21:27. What is the value of b?

    A) 12

    B) 35

    C) 64

    D) 107

23.

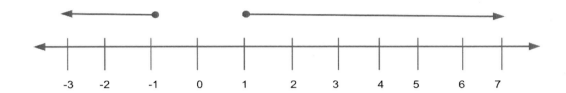

Which of the following describes the inequality graph above?

A) $-1 \leq x \ and \ x \geq 1$

B) $-1 \geq x \ and \ x \geq 1$

C) $-1 < x \ and \ x > 1$

D) $-1 < x \ and \ x > 1$

24. If $\frac{14}{2x+7} = 4$, what is x equal to?

A) $x = \frac{-7}{4}$

B) $x = \frac{7}{4}$

C) $x = \frac{5}{6}$

D) $x = \frac{3}{7}$

25. An aircraft carrier and a container ship left the port at the same time. They traveled in opposite directions. The container ship's velocity was 17 mph. After 10 hours, they were 320 miles apart. What was the speed of the aircraft carrier?

A) 25 mph

B) 15 mph

C) 5 mph

D) 23 mph

26. A brick has a height of 2 feet, a width of 3 feet, and a length of 3 feet. What is the volume of the brick, in inches?

    A) 18

    B) 216

    C) 2,592

    D) 31,104

27. Which of the following is a prime number?

    A) 23

    B) 32

    C) 39

    D) 45

28. What value of y makes $4(3) = \frac{6}{y} - 3$?

    A) $y = \frac{2}{5}$

    B) $y = \frac{3}{5}$

    C) $y = 4$

    D) $y = \frac{1}{2}$

29. How many pounds are in 5 ounces?

    A) $\frac{5}{16}$

    B) 0.5

    C) $\frac{16}{5}$

    D) 3.2

30. What is the value of the expression $\left(4(\frac{3}{4}+\frac{3}{7})\right)/9$?

    A) $\frac{17}{23}$

    B) $\frac{11}{21}$

    C) $\frac{9}{31}$

    D) $\frac{19}{22}$

31. An ice cream cone has a diameter of 4 inches and a height of 6 inches. If the formula of the volume of a cone is $V = \frac{1}{3}r^2h\pi$, what is its volume? Use $\pi = 3.14$. (Round to the nearest whole number)

    A) 25

    B) 27

    C) 100

    D) 101

32. If Annie is carrying a pitcher of water holding 2.4 liters of water and spills 40% of it by accident, how much water remains in the pitcher?

    A) 1.44 centiliters

    B) 0.004 kiloliters

    C) 14.4 deciliters

    D) 400 milliliters

33. If $40 = -10a + 7b$, what is the value of a in terms of b?

    A) $\frac{7}{10}b - 4 = a$

    B) $-3 + \frac{4}{7}b = a$

    C) $-4b + \frac{7}{10} = a$

    D) $\frac{4}{7} - 3b = a$

34. The triangle below is an isosceles triangle. What is the value of 2A - B?

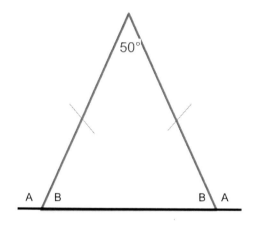

    A) 165

    B) 205

    C) 265

    D) 225

35. Find three consecutive numbers whose sum is 168. What is the value of the smallest number?

    A) 55

    B) 56

    C) 57

    D) 58

36. $\frac{5k-1}{5k-10} = \frac{7}{4}$

What is the value of k in the proportion above?

    A) $k = 4.4$

    B) $k = 3.5$

    C) $k = 9.2$

    D) $k = 1.2$

37. There are 3 algebra textbooks and 5 geometry textbooks. If algebra textbooks need to be placed on the top shelf and geometry textbooks need to be placed on the bottom shelf, how many different ways are there to arrange the books?

   A) 120

   B) 126

   C) 360

   D) 720

38. If 25% of x is equal to 5,500, what is x equal to?

   A) 1,375

   B) 2,750

   C) 11,000

   D) 22,000

39. In simplest form, what value of y makes $\frac{5y}{\sqrt{(2+7)}} = \frac{5}{2*3^2}$ true?

   A) y = 6

   B) $y = \frac{1}{6}$

   C) y = 5

   D) $y = \frac{1}{5}$

40. What is the prime factorization of 90?

   A) $10 * 3^2$

   B) $2 * 3^2 * 5$

   C) $2 * 3 * 5$

   D) $2^2 * 3^2 * 5$

41. Two identical circles are inscribed onto a rectangle. If each circle has an area of 16π square inches, what is the area of rectangle ABCD?

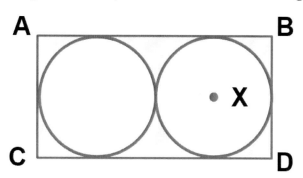

A) 16 square inches

B) 32 square inches

C) 48 square inches

D) 128 square inches

42. $\frac{4}{8} = \frac{x-6}{5x+1}$

What is the value of x in the proportion above? (Round to the nearest hundredth)

A) $x = -3.65$

B) $x = -1.67$

C) $x = -2.25$

D) $x = -4.33$

43. What is the value of the expression $\frac{5}{6}x + \frac{8}{5}$ if $x = \frac{3}{5}$?

A) $\frac{21}{10}$

B) $\frac{17}{7}$

C) $\frac{13}{5}$

D) $\frac{21}{9}$

44. What is the value of angle a?

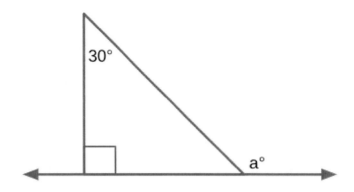

    A) 60°

    B) 90°

    C) 100°

    D) 120°

45. Joe's pencil case has 10 blue pens, 7 black pens, 4 red pens, and 6 green pens. What is the probability of Joe not choosing a green pen?

    A) $\frac{8}{27}$

    B) $\frac{6}{27}$

    C) $\frac{7}{9}$

    D) $\frac{1}{3}$

46. What is the value of x in $\frac{2x}{5^2-11} = \frac{7}{x}$?

    A) x = 5

    B) x = 14

    C) x = 7

    D) x = 9

47. Victor pays $2.75 for 5 pencils and 3 erasers. Kia pays $3.50 for 2 pencils and 6 erasers. What is the cost of one pencil?

    A) $0.10

    B) $0.25

    C) $0.50

    D) $.75

48. Which of the following cannot be the area of a square, if all the sides of the square are integers?

    A) 4

    B) 6

    C) 9

    D) 16

49. The price of a shoe had been $300. After a couple months, the price increased by 40%. If Brian's credit card allows him to get it for 20% off, what is the new price of the shoe?

    A) 312

    B) 336

    C) 354

    D) 366

50. A man is 6 feet 3 inches. How many yards tall is he? Round to the nearest hundredth.

    A) 2.08 yards

    B) 2.75 yards

    C) 3.25 yards

    D) 3.81 yards

51. Between which two consecutive integers is $\frac{88}{9}$?

    A) 6 and 7

    B) 7 and 8

    C) 8 and 9

    D) 9 and 10

52. If $\frac{7x}{2} + \frac{y}{3} = 4$, what is y in terms of x?

    A) $y = 32 - \frac{3x}{6}$

    B) $y = -\frac{3x}{2} + 15$

    C) $y = 12 - \frac{21x}{2}$

    D) $y = -\frac{7x}{2} - 12$

53. Let $a = \frac{7}{13}$, $b = \frac{4}{7}$, and $c = \frac{5}{9}$, then

    A) a < b < c

    B) a < c < b

    C) b < c < a

    D) b < a < c

54. A tube of glue costs \$3.50 and a piece of felt costs \$1.75. If you bought one tube of glue, which of the following inequalities represent the maximum amount of felt that could be bought with \$10?

    A) $10 > 3.50 + 1.75x$

    B) $10 \leq 3.50 + 1.75x$

    C) $10 \geq 3.50 + 1.75x$

    D) $10 < 3.50 + 1.75x$

55. What is the value of m if $5(1-m) - 2(1-m) = 15$?

    A) m = 3

    B) m = 9

    C) m = −2

    D) m = −4

SHSAT Mathematics Practice Test #5:

1. Ben deposits $5,000 into a savings account that has 8% simple interest every two years. How much money is in the account at the end of 8 years?

2. What is the value of y in the equation $-3(y-1) + 8(y-3) = 6y + 7 - 5y$?

3.

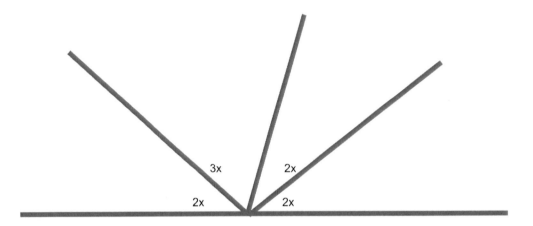

In the diagram above, what is the measure of x?

4. When x is divided by 6, the quotient is 7, and the remainder is 4. When x is divided by 4, the quotient is Q, and the remainder is z. What is the value of z?

5. If A is (-2,4) and B is (8,20), what is the sum of the x coordinate and y coordinate of the midpoint of AB?

6. What is the least common multiple of 28 and 48?

   A) 96

   B) 128

   C) 336

   D) 398

7. If $\frac{1}{3}a + \frac{3}{4}b = 21$, what is the value of b in terms of a?

   A) $b = -3 + \frac{4}{3}a$

   B) $b = 28 - \frac{4}{9}a$

   C) $b = -13 - \frac{5}{3}a$

   D) $b = 20 + \frac{7}{9}a$

8. If x is an even integer, which of the following must be an even number?

   A) 2x

   B) 3x + 1

   C) 4x + 5

   D) 5x - 3

9. Dean left the museum and started driving west. Jack left two hours later, and he drove 30 mph **faster** to try to catch up to Dean. He caught up after 3 hours. What was Dean's average speed?

   A) 11 mph

   B) 18 mph

   C) 45 mph

   D) 60 mph

10. In the equation $x + 2y = -2y - (x + 14)$, what is the value of x if $y = -5$?

    A) $x = \frac{-1}{3}$

    B) $x = -3$

    C) $x = \frac{1}{3}$

    D) $x = 3$

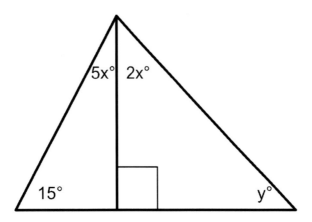

11.

    In the diagram above, what is the value of y?

    A) 15

    B) 20

    C) 30

    D) 60

12. Terrance wants to go golfing every 8th week. How many times will he go golfing in 2 years?

    A) 13

    B) 14

    C) 15

    D) 16

13. On Chris's farm, there are three different types of animals. The farm has 60 pigs. There are 15% more chickens than pigs. There are also five fewer cows than pigs. If a random animal ran away, what is the percentage possibility that the animal would be a cow?

    A) $\frac{55}{184}$

    B) $\frac{65}{184}$

    C) $\frac{33}{92}$

    D) $\frac{45}{92}$

14. Solve the inequality: $4x + 7 < 35$

    A) $x < 6$

    B) $x < 7$

    C) $x \leq 6$

    D) $x \leq 7$

15. What is 8.375 written as a fraction?

    A) $\frac{67}{8}$

    B) $\frac{139}{16}$

    C) $\frac{72}{6}$

    D) $\frac{55}{7}$

16. If the diameter of a sphere is 18cm, approximately what is the volume of the sphere? Use $\pi = 3.14$. Round to the nearest whole number.

    A) $2{,}541\ cm^3$

    B) $2{,}786\ cm^3$

    C) $3{,}054\ cm^3$

    D) $24{,}429\ cm^3$

17. What is the value of n in the equation $0.25(n + 8) = 15$?

    A) n = 26

    B) n = 7

    C) n = 36

    D) n = 52

18. A steel cube with an initial temperature of 20 C° is put into a freezer. Every hour, the steel cube's temperature decreases by 3 F°. If the cube was left in the freezer for 4.5 hours, what was its final temperature, in Fahrenheit? Use the formula, $(C \times \frac{9}{5}) + 32 = F$.

    A) 10.3 F°

    B) 54.5 F°

    C) 61.2 F°

    D) 82.4 F°

19. If $\sqrt{9x} = 6$, what is the value of x?

    A) 4

    B) 5

    C) 6

    D) 7

20. The sum of 5 consecutive integers equals 6 times the smallest integer. Find the largest integer.

    A) 11

    B) 12

    C) 13

    D) 14

21. Solve the inequality:

-5x + 22 < 3x - 2

    A) x < 3

    B) x > 3

    C) x ≤ 3

    D) $x \geq 3$

22. $-\dfrac{9}{2k-10} = \dfrac{6}{2k+5}$

What is the value of k in the proportion above?

    A) $k = 0.5$

    B) $k = 6.1$

    C) $k = -4$

    D) $k = -3.7$

23. What is the value of the expression: $2(\frac{3}{4} + \frac{7}{9}) * (\frac{1}{2})^2$?

    A) $\frac{55}{18}$

    B) $\frac{55}{72}$

    C) $\frac{110}{79}$

    D) $\frac{59}{21}$

24. What is the surface area of a sphere with a height of 12 inches? Use $\pi=3.14$.

    A) 153.57 square inches

    B) 342.68 square inches

    C) 452.16 square inches

    D) 480.32 square inches

25. What is the value of x in the equation below?

$$x^2(4 + y) = 20$$

    A) $x = \sqrt{5y}$

    B) $x = \sqrt{\dfrac{5}{y}}$

    C) $x = \sqrt{\dfrac{20}{4+y}}$

    D) $x = \sqrt{5 + \dfrac{20}{y}}$

26. Mary has 32 friends. All of her friends each have a vehicle. ½ of her friends have a bicycle. ¼ of her friends own a unicycle. The rest own a tricycle. How many wheels are there in total?

    A) 36

    B) 48

    C) 56

    D) 64

27. B is the supplementary angle to a. If b is equal to $\frac{1}{2}a - 6$, what are the values of angles a and b?

    A) ∠a=142 and ∠b=38

    B) ∠a=135 and ∠b=45

    C) ∠a=124 and ∠b=56

    D) ∠a=117 and ∠b=63

28. What is the integer value of x in $|5x + 37| = 12$?

    A) x = -5

    B) x = -7

    C) x = -13

    D) x = -2

29.   Having researched the value of houses in his neighborhood, Tony discovered that 2 houses are worth less than $400,000, 5 houses are worth $400,000 - $600,000, 8 houses are $600,000 - $800,000, and 10 houses are worth more than $800,000. Approximately what percent of houses are worth more than $600,000?

    A) 40%

    B) 72%

    C) 64%

    D) 60%

30. A baker pours ingredients A, B, and C, into a bowl. The ratio of amount of A to amount B is 1:2, and the ratio of amount B to C is 3:4. How many times bigger is amount C than amount A?

    A) $2\frac{2}{3}$

    B) $1\frac{1}{6}$

    C) $3\frac{5}{12}$

    D) $4\frac{11}{12}$

31. $-3(1-3x) + 7(3+6x) = 18$

    What is the value of x in the equation above?

    A) $x = -15$

    B) *No solutions*

    C) $x = 0$

    D) $x = 1$

32. Which of the following has a slope that is the reciprocal of $\frac{2}{5}$ and passes through the point (2,2)?

    A) $y = \frac{2}{5}x - 1$

    B) $y = \frac{5}{2}x - 3$

    C) $y = \frac{2}{5}x$

    D) $y = \frac{5}{2}x - 2$

33. What is the value of a in the equation below?

$$(4a - 2b) - 3(a - 2) = -62$$

A) $a = -56 + b$

B) $a = 21 - \dfrac{b}{2}$

C) $a = 2b - 68$

D) $a = -3b + 41$

34. What is the solution to the systems of equations below?

$$7x - 2y = 23$$

$$x + 2y = 17$$

A) $(2, -5)$

B) $(5, 5)$

C) $(-2, 4)$

D) $(5, 6)$

35. The sum of two consecutive integers is 133. What is the largest number?

A) 63

B) 65

C) 67

D) 71

36. If the sides of triangle ABC are 2.5 times bigger than the sides of triangle XYZ, what is the area of triangle XYZ?

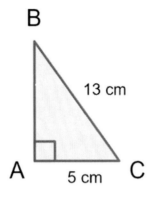
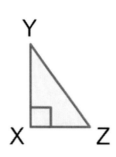

A) 0.6 sq cm

B) 1.8 sq cm

C) 3.2 sq cm

D) 4.8 sq cm

37.

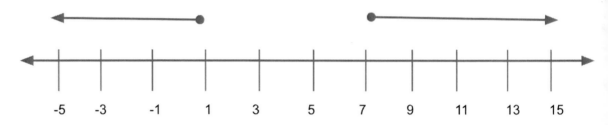

Which of the following inequalities represents the graph above?

A) $1 < x$ and $x > 7$

B) $1 \geq x$ and $x \geq 7$

C) $1 < x$ or $x > 7$

D) $1 > x$ or $x > 7$

38. How many positive integers of 5 digits may be made from the ciphers 2,4,5,8, and 9 if each digit can only be used once?

    A) 20

    B) 60.

    C) 120

    D) 180

39. What is the value of x in $-2(x + 8) - 7(x - 1) = -6x$?

    A) x = -3

    B) x = -5

    C) x = 6

    D) x = 2

40. Emily has $300 in her wallet and Jena has $500 in her wallet. Both donate 30% of the money in their wallet to a charity. What is the total amount of money they donated?

    A) $90

    B) $180

    C) $210

    D) $240

41. What is the value of a in terms of b and c?

$$3(a + 3c) + 12 = 6b$$

    A) $b + c + 1$

    B) $2b - 3c - 4$

    C) $6b - 2c + 3$

    D) $4b - c + 6$

42. Solve for x:

$|-2x+3| > 11$

   A) $-4 \geq x \geq 7$

   B) $-4 \geq x$ or $x \leq 7$

   C) $-4 < x < 7$

   D) $-4 > x$ or $x < 7$

43. A person runs at a rate of 3 feet per minute. How many hours does it take to run 60 yards?

   A) 1

   B) 2

   C) 3

   D) 4

44. If the pentagon below is a regular pentagon, what is the value of x?

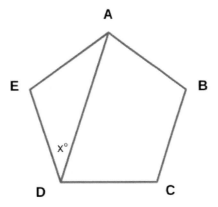

   A) 25°

   B) 36°

   C) 75°

   D) 82°

45. What is the value of $3\frac{1}{9} \div 1\frac{3}{4}$?

    A) $\frac{5}{12}$

    B) $1\frac{7}{9}$

    C) $2\frac{5}{36}$

    D) $3\frac{1}{6}$

46. What is the value of $\dfrac{6^5}{6^{-3} * 6^{-2}}$?

    A) 6^{10}

    B) 1

    C) 6^{-10}

    D) -1

47. What is the value of x in $25x + 17(x - 6) = x(12)^2$?

    A) x = 14

    B) x = -8

    C) x = 21

    D) x = -1

48. When a is divided by 9, the quotient is 6 and the remainder is 7. When a is divided by 4, the quotient is q and the remainder is b. What is q x b?

    A) 1

    B) 15

    C) 9

    D) 7

49. A rectangular hole has a length of 0.032 kilometer and a width of 1,600 centimeters. If the volume of the hole is 1,024 cubic meters, what is the depth of the hole?

    A) 0.2 meters

    B) 2 meters

    C) 20 meters

    D) 200 meters

50. If $\frac{2}{3}x = 50$, what is the value of 5x?

    A) 50

    B) 75

    C) 225

    D) 375

51. $-4(x - 2) < 4$

    What is the solution to the inequality above?

    A) x < 1

    B) x < -1

    C) x > 1

    D) x > -1

52. $\frac{7x-2}{5} = \frac{x}{5}$

    What is the value of x needed to make the proportion above true? (Round to the nearest tenth)

    A) $x = -0.3$

    B) $x = 2.7$

    C) $x = 7.2$

    D) $x = 0.3$

53. What is the value of x in the picture below?

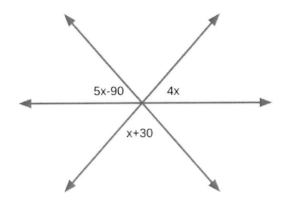

5x-90   4x

x+30

A) 24

B) 62

C) 98

D) 120

54. What is the solution to the system of equations below?

$$-7x + 8y = 9$$
$$9x - 8y = -7$$

A) $(1,8)$

B) $(8,-9)$

C) $(8,10)$

D) $(1,2)$

55. If $\frac{2}{y} = -x^2 + 4z - 24$, what is z in terms of x and y?

A) $2x^2 - 2y - 15 = z$

B) $\frac{x^2}{4} + \frac{1}{2y} + 6 = z$

C) $\frac{x^2}{8} + \frac{3}{y} - 1 = z$

D) $\frac{5x^2}{6} - 2y + 3 = z$

SHSAT Mathematics Practice Test #6:

1. In a tournament, there is a first-place prize and a second-place prize. 4 people bought tickets. How many ways can the prizes be handed out?

2.

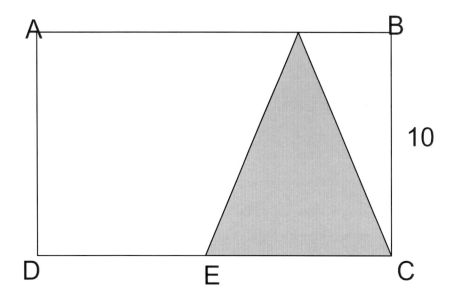

The figure above is rectangle ABCD, whose longer sides are twice as large as its shorter side. E is a midpoint on side DC. What is the area of the shaded region, if side BC is 10 units long? (Not drawn to scale).

3. In the infinitely repeating decimal, *0.384615384615*, what is the 22nd digit?

4. What is the area of the shaded section?

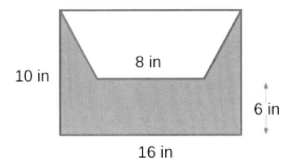

5. What is the value of x? (Figure is not drawn to scale)

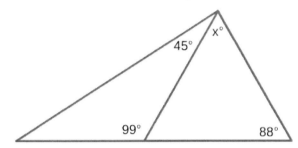

6. For what value of n does $24 + 8n = 8(5n + 8) + 8n$?

    A) n = 4

    B) n = 2

    C) n = -1

    D) n = -9

7. The product of two consecutive, positive, and even integers times 6 equals 288. Find the two consecutive integers.

    A) 4,6

    B) 8,10

    C) 7,9

    D) 6,8

8. Which of the following is equal to 40% of $\frac{8}{5}$?

    A) 0.25

    B) 0.64

    C) 0.96

    D) 1.02

9. What is the distance from (3,4) to (-7,-2)?

    A) $\sqrt{151}$

    B) $\sqrt{136}$

    C) $\sqrt{166}$

    D) $\sqrt{174}$

10. Which of the following is the solution to the inequality below?

$7(x+6) \leq 56$

    A) $[-\infty, \infty]$

    B) $[2, \infty)$

    C) $[-2, \infty]$

    D) $(-\infty, 2]$

11. A class door has a width of 45 centimeters, a height of 110 centimeters, and a length of 84 centimeters. What is the surface area of the door in meters?

    A) 3.177

    B) 3.342

    C) 3.594

    D) 3.751

12. In the equation, $5.5(7.9k - 11.6) = 5.8(k + 7.9) - 9.6k$, what is the value of k?

    A) $k = -2.4$

    B) $k = 2.32$

    C) $k = -8.74$

    D) $k = 5.2$

13. Patrick and Neil are running a 9 mile race. If Patrick runs at a rate of 0.075 miles per minute and Neil runs at a rate of 3 miles per hour, who will win the race? By how much will that person win the race?

    A) Patrick will win by 1 hour.

    B) Patrick will win by 1.5 hours.

    C) Neil will win by 1 hour.

    D) Neil will win by 1.5 hours.

14. If Ben flips a coin four times, what is the chance of the coin landing on tails all four times?

  A) $\frac{1}{2}$

  B) $\frac{1}{4}$

  C) $\frac{1}{8}$

  D) $\frac{1}{16}$

15. Face A of the rectangular prism, below, has an area of 195 sq cm, and Face B has an area of 65 sq cm. What is the ratio of the largest length of the rectangular prism to the smallest length of the rectangular prism?

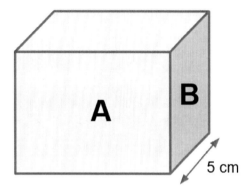

  A) 2:1

  B) 5:1

  C) 4:3

  D) 3:1

16. What is the least common multiple of 12, 14, and 21?

  A) 42

  B) 84

  C) 72

  D) 98

17. What is the value of n if $\frac{65}{n} = 0.0065$?

    A) n = 10,000

    B) n = 100,000

    C) n = 1,000,000

    D) n = 10,000,000

18. A restaurant offering all-you-can-eat dinner has 48 customers in one night. The cost of a meal for an adult is $30 and the cost of a meal for a child is $15. If the restaurant earned $1,245 that night, how many adults and children attended the restaurant that night?

    A) 27 adults and 21 children

    B) 31 adults and 17 children

    C) 35 adults and 13 children

    D) 40 adults and 8 children

19. On a map, 1 yard is represented by 4 inches. How many inches is 1 foot on the map?

    A) 1 inches

    B) $\frac{1}{2}$ inches

    C) $\frac{3}{4}$ inches

    D) $1\frac{1}{3}$ inches

20. $\frac{n}{6} = \frac{n-9}{2}$.

    Rounding to the nearest tenth, what is the value of n in the equation above?

    A) $n = 9.9$

    B) $n = -8.3$

    C) $n = 13.5$

    D) $n = -12.6$

21. What is the value of y in $\frac{0.21}{0.33} = \frac{y}{1.10}$?

    A) y = 0.7

    B) y = 0.66

    C) y = 0.64

    D) y = 0.55

22.

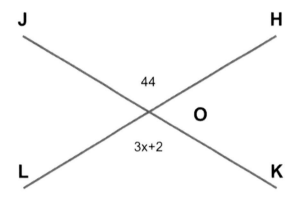

In the diagram above, what is the value of 2x?

    A) 5

    B) 7

    C) 14

    D) 28

23. What are the two consecutive integers that add up to 145?

    A) 71 and 72

    B) 72 and 73

    C) 73 and 74

    D) 74 and 75

24. John has 220 apples, which is $\frac{4}{3}$ times more apples than Lisa has. How many more apples does John have than Lisa?

    A) 25

    B) 55

    C) 195

    D) 230

25. Shirley has a rectangular piece of fabric that is 16 inches long and 12 inches wide. For a project, she cuts out a circle with a radius of 4 inches. How much fabric does Shirley have left? Use π=3.14.

    A) 94.67 sq in

    B) 141.76 sq in

    C) 160.89 sq in

    D) 294.75 sq in

26. $\frac{8^2}{2^7}$ is equivalent to which of the following?

    A) 0.25

    B) 0.5

    C) 0.125

    D) 0.75

27. Aveline left her house and drove towards the river at an average speed of *40* km/h. Jessica left sometime later traveling in the same direction at an average speed of *60* km/h. After traveling for *2* hours, Jessica caught up with Avelina. How many hours did Avelina travel before Jessica caught up with her?

    A) *5* hours

    B) *3* hours

    C) *7* hours

    D) *4* hours

28. What is the value of x in the diagram below?

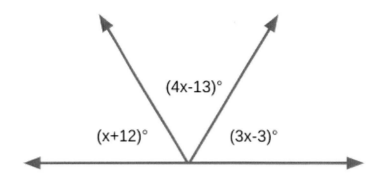

A) 12

B) 23

C) 36

D) 49

29. When $3a(a + 3) - (b - 1) = 64$, what is the value of b in terms of a?

A) $3a^2 - 4a - 42 = b$

B) $a^2 + 2a - 21 = b$

C) $a^2 - 2a + 21 = b$

D) $3a^2 + 9a - 63 = b$

30. What is the solution to the system of equations below?

$$-21 - 4x = -y$$
$$-3y - 7 - 2x = 0$$

A) $(-5,1)$

B) $(5,-1)$

C) $(-5,-1)$

D) $(-8,1)$

31.

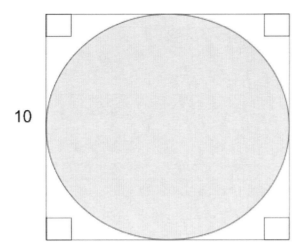

10

The figure above is a square whose side is 10. Find the area of the shaded region.

A) 50π

B) 100π

C) 25π

D) 5π

32. There are 20 marbles in a bag. 4 marbles are red, 11 marbles are blue, and 5 marbles are green. What is the probability someone will draw a red marble and the second draw will be green, if they put the first marble back into the bag?

A) $\frac{1}{20}$

B) $\frac{1}{9}$

C) $\frac{9}{20}$

D) $\frac{2}{20}$

33. What is the value of x in the equation below?

$$\frac{8x + 4}{7} = 12$$

  A) 10

  B) 11

  C) 12

  D) 13

34. There is a jug that contains 1.5 gallons of juice. Billy drinks 4 cups of juice. Sandra drinks 10% of what's left in the jug. How much juice is left in the jug?

  A) 2 cups

  B) 12 cups

  C) 18 cups

  D) 22 cups

35. What is the value of the expression $4[2(\frac{1}{2} - \frac{1}{3})]^2$?

  A) $\frac{2}{3}$

  B) $\frac{4}{9}$

  C) $\frac{5}{9}$

  D) $\frac{7}{9}$

36. $\frac{-94+x}{16} = 5y + 2$. What is the value of x if $y = -2$?

  A) -64

  B) -34

  C) 36

  D) 27

37. What is the greatest common factor between 85, 170, and 374?

    A) 85

    B) 17

    C) 19

    D) 12

38. Lines $\underline{VW}$ and $\underline{YX}$ are parallel. If $\angle 1$ is equal to $\frac{3}{4}x + 16$ and $\angle 6$ is equal to $2x -$ 34, what is the value of $\angle 3$?

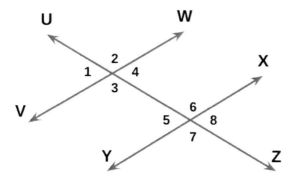

    A) 70°

    B) 110°

    C) 51°

    D) 129°

39. Which of the following is an inequality that represents four times a number plus 25 is more than a number over 2?

    A) $4x - 25 > \frac{x}{2}$

    B) $4x + 25 < \frac{x}{2}$

    C) $4x + 25 > \frac{x}{2}$

    D) $4x - 25 < \frac{x}{2}$

40. What is the midpoint of (25,42) and (41,54)?

  A) (32,46)

  B) (34,48)

  C) (26,48)

  D) (33,48)

41. $-\dfrac{11}{a-2} = \dfrac{4}{5}$

  What is the value of a in the proportion above?

  A) $a = -9.8$

  B) $a = 1.2$

  C) $a = 4$

  D) $a = -11.75$

42. What is the value of b in terms of a?

$$\frac{7}{8}a = 14b - 3$$

  A) $\dfrac{1}{4}a + \dfrac{3}{8} = b$

  B) $\dfrac{3}{8}a + \dfrac{3}{16} = b$

  C) $\dfrac{3}{2}a + \dfrac{5}{16} = b$

  D) $\dfrac{1}{16}a + \dfrac{3}{14} = b$

43. The smallest positive value of x that will make 7x divisible by 42 without a remainder is which of the following?

  A) 10

  B) 12

  C) 14

  D) 16

44. What is the perimeter of a circle with a diameter of 24.4 feet? Use π=3.14. Round to the nearest hundredths if needed.

    A) 64.51 feet

    B) 76.62 feet

    C) 82.68 feet

    D) 96.78 feet

45. If 5 feet is equal to 1.524 meters, how many centimeters are in a foot? Round to the nearest hundredth place.

    A) 0.31 centimeters

    B) 3.05 centimeters

    C) 30.84 centimeters

    D) 30.48 centimeters

46. If a = $\sqrt{28}$, what is the value of $(a)^3$?

    A) 28

    B) $14\sqrt{7}$

    C) $28\sqrt{7}$

    D) $56\sqrt{7}$

47. A can is 5 inches tall. If the can lid is 5 inches wide, what is the volume of the can? Use π=3.14.

    A) 63.425 cubic inches

    B) 74.861 cubic inches

    C) 98.125 cubic inches

    D) 124.520 cubic inches

48. If x = 3, which of the following equations are true?

   A) $x^2 + 4 = 14$

   B) $x^3 - 5 = 22$

   C) x -2 = 2

   D) |x-7| * 4 = -16

49. Eugene left Daniel's home and traveled toward the sea at an average speed of 40 km/h. Daniel left some time later, driving in the opposite direction with an average speed of 50 km/h. After Eugene had driven for 4 hours, they were 360 km apart. How many hours did Daniel drive?

   A) 3 hours

   B) 4 hours

   C) 5 hours

   D) 2 hours

50. What is the slope of (5,-6) and (-6,5)?

   A) 1

   B) -1

   C) $\frac{-1}{11}$

   D) $\frac{1}{11}$

51.

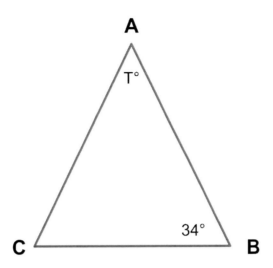

In the diagram above, if angle T equals 78 degrees, what is the measure of angle C?

    A) 66
    B) 67
    C) 68
    D) 69

52. Matty rents a moving truck. He has to pay a flat fee of $20, in addition to being charged $3.50 per hour. If Matty is willing to pay a maximum of $41, what is the greatest number of hours for which he can rent the truck?

    A) 4
    B) 5
    C) 6
    D) 7

53. A concert happens exactly once every 15 days. How many times will the concert happen over half a year?

    A) *14*

    B) *11*

    C) *12*

    D) *16*

54. What is the value of 3x?

$$3x - 15 = 2y$$

    A) 2y+15

    B) $\frac{1}{2}y + 5$

    C) y+5

    D) $\frac{3}{4}y + 4$

55. An average American generates about 5 pounds of trash each day. One big heavy duty trash bag can hold 10 pounds of trash. What percent of the bag would be filled when only 6 hours of the day have gone by?

    A) 12.5 %

    B) 25%

    C) 50%

    D) 75%

SHSAT Mathematics Practice Test #7:

1. A patient is prescribed a dosage of 12 mg of a certain drug per day and is allowed to refill his prescription twice. If there are 60 tablets in a prescription, and each tablet has 4 mg, how many doses can the patient have in total?

2. What is the value of d in the system of equations below?

$$\frac{c - 8}{2} + \frac{d + 6}{3} = -3$$

$$2c - 6d = -26$$

3. What is the value of x in the equation $x - 4 = \frac{x}{2}$?

4. A = {9,53,44,18,14,20,77}
   B = {45,66,3,17,33,24,55}
   What is the difference in the median between set B and set A?

5.

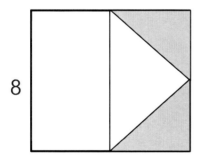

E, G, and F are midpoints of the sides of square ABCD, shown above. What is the sum of the areas of the shaded triangles?

6. $\dfrac{p-5}{9} = \dfrac{p}{5}$

What is the value of p in the proportion shown above? (Round to the nearest hundredth)

    A) $p = -4.33$

    B) $p = -6.25$

    C) $p = 5.13$

    D) $p = -6.67$

7. The reciprocal of 0.625 is subtracted from the reciprocal of $\frac{1}{2}$. What is the reciprocal of this difference?

    A) $\dfrac{5}{3}$

    B) $\dfrac{5}{2}$

    C) $\dfrac{3}{5}$

    D) $\dfrac{2}{5}$

8. A rectangular pyramid has a length of 5 cm, a width of 6 cm, and a volume of 80 cubic centimeters. What is the height?

    A) 7 cm

    B) 8 cm

    C) 9 cm

    D) 10 cm

9. The sum of three consecutive, odd integers is 45. What is the product of the smallest and largest number?

    A) 143

    B) 197

    C) 221

    D) 245

10. Omar, Adrian and Jon are running a race. Omar runs 3x+14 number of miles. Adrian runs 3 miles less than half of Omar's number of miles. If Jon runs twice the amount Omar and Adrian ran combined, what is the number of miles Jon ran, in terms of x?

   A) $2x + 28$

   B) $9x + 36$

   C) $4x + 24$

   D) $3x + 18$

11. $5(.02)^2 + 5.01 - 5(.02) =$

   A) 4.911

   B) 4.912

   C) 4.913

   D) 4.914

12. Which of the following is the smallest factor of 4056?

   A) 22

   B) 23

   C) 24

   D) 25

13. A package weighs 2 kilograms over the weight limit. If the weight limit is 20 pounds, what is the weight of the package? (Use $2.2lb = 1kg$)

   A) $15.6 \, lb$

   B) $24.4 \, lb$

   C) $22.0 \, lb$

   D) $14.0 \, lb$

14. What is the value of $\frac{5(5+3)}{8} + \frac{17}{32}$?

    A) $\frac{159}{16}$

    B) $\frac{29}{8}$

    C) $\frac{177}{32}$

    D) $\frac{197}{32}$

15. If angle y is equal to $\frac{1}{3}a + 12$, what is the value of a?

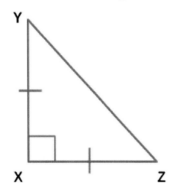

    A) 99

    B) 108

    C) 165

    D) 201

16. Which of the following is a number that is a possible solution to the inequality below?

$$-\frac{17}{4} < x < -\frac{22}{7}$$

    A) -7

    B) -6

    C) -5

    D) -4

17. In the equation $\frac{9}{2n} = \frac{3y}{8}$, what is the value of n if $y = 6$?

    A) n = 1

    B) n = 2

    C) n = 3

    D) n = 5

18. What is the least common multiple of 5, 12, and 27?

    A) 810

    B) 540

    C) 1620

    D) 2520

19. The figure below depicts a semicircle and a triangle. What is the area of the two figures? Use π=3.14.

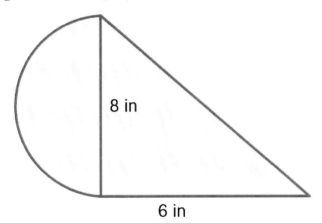

    A) 49.12 sq in

    B) 64.24 sq in

    C) 86.35 sq in

    D) 174.72 sq in

20. What is the difference between x and y in the system of equations below?

$$4x + 8y = -4$$
$$6x - 4y = 6$$

A) $\frac{1}{2}$

B) $\frac{2}{3}$

C) 1

D) $\frac{5}{4}$

21. What is the value of x in $-2(-7x - 8) = -39 + 3x$?

A) x = -5

B) x = -7

C) x = -2

D) x = -4

22. A pencil case has 80 pens that are either red, black, or blue. The ratio of red to black is 8:7, and the ratio of black to blue is 7:5. If 3 blacks pens are removed, what is the probability of choosing a black pen from the pencil case?

A) $\frac{1}{2}$

B) $\frac{25}{77}$

C) $\frac{1}{3}$

D) $\frac{25}{80}$

23. Which of the following equations is parallel to 2y = 4x + 8?

A) y = -2x + 7

B) 4y = 8x + 9

C) y = 4x - 11

D) 4y = 2x + C

24. John purchased 8 gallons of water for a camping trip and plans to pour all of the water into insulated flasks that measure 1 quart each to keep the water cool. How many flasks will it take to contain all 8 gallons?

   A) *12* flasks

   B) *16* flasks

   C) *32* flasks

   D) *64* flasks

25. $(\frac{8^3 \times 8^{12}}{8^3})^2 =$

   A) 8^7

   B) 8^8

   C) 8^{10}

   D) 8^{24}

26. In a rectangle, the length of the shorter and longer side is two consecutive numbers that equal 19. What is the perimeter of the rectangle?

   A) 32

   B) 34

   C) 36

   D) 38

27. What is 250% of 120?

   A) 180

   B) 240

   C) 280

   D) 300

28. A rectangular prism has a height of 5 units, a length of 3 units, and a width of 4 units. What is the total surface area?

    A) 78

    B) 94

    C) 114

    D) 126

29. If $2a^2 + 64 = b$, what is a in terms of b?

    A) $a = \sqrt{(\frac{1}{2}b - 32)}$

    B) $a = \sqrt{(b - 32)}$

    C) $a = \sqrt{(b - 21)}$

    D) $a = \sqrt{(\frac{1}{2}b - 21)}$

30. The average of five consecutive odd integers is 11. What is the middle number?

    A) 9

    B) 11

    C) 13

    D) 15

31. Shaun left the airport and traveled toward the train station at an average speed of 45 km/h. Mark left the airport some time later, traveling in the opposite direction of the train station with an average speed of 70 km/h. After Shaun had traveled for 4 hours, they were 320 km apart. Find the time it took Mark to arrive at the airport.

    A) 2 hours

    B) 4 hours

    C) 3 hours

    D) 1 hou

32. What is the slope of a line that is perpendicular to -5x + 8y = 26?

    A) $-\frac{5}{8}$

    B) $\frac{8}{5}$

    C) $\frac{5}{8}$

    D) $-\frac{8}{5}$

33. What is the value of x in $\sqrt{(x^3)} - 12 = 2(5) + 1 + 3(4 - 9)$?

    A) $x = 2$

    B) $x = 4$

    C) $x = 9$

    D) $x = 16$

34.

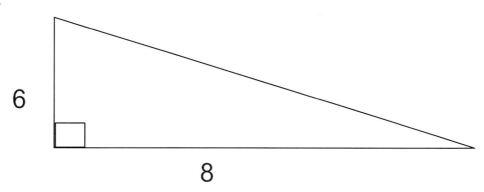

The figure above is a right triangle whose sides are given, what is the perimeter of the whole triangle?

    A) $14\ cm^2$

    B) $17\ cm^2$

    C) $24\ cm^2$

    D) $12\ cm^2$

35. What is the value of the expression $\frac{2(6+3)}{\sqrt{36}} / \frac{2}{9}$?

    A) $\frac{27}{2}$

    B) $\frac{27}{4}$

    C) $\frac{12}{7}$

    D) $\frac{9}{29}$

36. A jogger accidentally spills 60% of the water in her half-full bottle. If the bottle has a total capacity of 2 liters, how much water is left after the spill?

    A) 0.80 L

    B) 0.60 L

    C) 0.25 L

    D) 0.40 L

37. Andrew and Pete went flower picking. They found that 16 of the flowers they picked only had 8 petals. They also found that 20 flowers had 5 petals and 14 of the flowers had 12 petals. What would be the mode of the number of petals?

    A) 20 petals

    B) 5 petals

    C) 8 petals

    D) 12 petals

38. Which of the following is a possible solution to x?

    $\frac{1}{2} < x < \frac{1}{3}$

    A) 0.48

    B) 0.55

    C) 0.67

    D) 0.72

39. If $a = \frac{1}{2}(4b - 5)$, what is 3b?

  A) $\frac{3}{2}a + \frac{15}{4}$

  B) $2a + \frac{5}{2}$

  C) $\frac{1}{2}a + \frac{5}{4}$

  D) $a + \frac{3}{2}$

40. The area of the parallelogram is 220 square inches, line AB = 2(x-3), and line BC = x+2. What is the value of x?

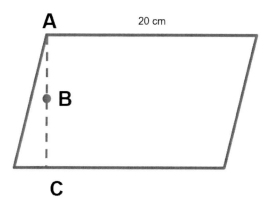

  A) 5
  B) 6
  C) 7
  D) 8

41. Which of the following points on the coordinate plane is 5 units away from (2,2)?

  A) (3,5)
  B) (5,6)
  C) (6,2)
  D) (4,4)

42. Computer A costs $500. It is on sale for 30% off, and the customer has a $10 off coupon. Computer B costs $600. It is on sale for 40% off, but the customer does not have a coupon. What is the new price of computer A compared to computer B?

    A) $20, cheaper

    B) $30, cheaper

    C) $20, greater

    D) $30, greater

43. Emily left her apartment building and traveled toward the next city over at an average speed of 20 mph. Some time later, Leah left the same building, and traveled in the same direction at an average speed of 24 mph. After traveling for 5 hours, Leah caught up with Emily. How much time did Emily travel for before Leah caught up with her?

    A) 6 hours

    B) 7 hours

    C) 9 hours

    D) 8 hours

44. What is the value of x in $x - |47 - 74| + |132 - 231| = 28$?

    A) x = 44

    B) x = 53

    C) x = -44

    D) x = -36

45.

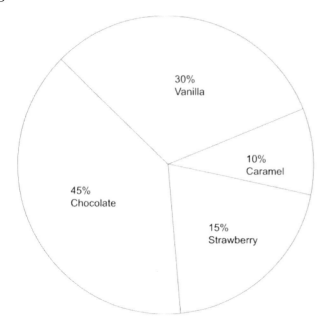

30%
Vanilla

10%
Caramel

45%
Chocolate

15%
Strawberry

There are 20,000 teens whose favorite ice cream is caramel. How many teens say that their favorite flavor is chocolate?

   A) 45,000

   B) 90,000

   C) 30,000

   D) 25,000

46. If a regular polygon has exterior angles of 45°, what shape is the regular polygon?

   A) Pentagon

   B) Hexagon

   C) Heptagon

   D) Octagon

47. If y = 4x + 3, what is the value of x in 2x + y = 33?

    A) 2

    B) 3

    C) 4

    D) 5

48. Between which two consecutive integers is $\frac{74}{12}$?

    A) 6 and 7

    B) 7 and 8

    C) 8 and 9

    D) 9 and 10

49. What is the greatest common factor of 66 and 84?

    A) 12

    B) 6

    C) 9

    D) 18

50. What is the value of a in terms of b and c?

$$8a + 2b + 3c = 180$$

    A) $a = \frac{65}{4} - \frac{1}{4}b - \frac{3}{8}c$

    B) $a = 18 - \frac{1}{8}b + \frac{1}{4}c$

    C) $a = \frac{65}{4} - \frac{1}{8}b + \frac{1}{4}c$

    D) $a = \frac{45}{2} - \frac{1}{4}b - \frac{3}{8}c$

51. $\sqrt{72} - \sqrt{48}$

    A) $6\sqrt{2} - 4\sqrt{3}$

    B) $4\sqrt{2} - 2\sqrt{3}$

    C) $6\sqrt{2} - 6\sqrt{3}$

    D) $6\sqrt{2} + 4\sqrt{3}$

52.

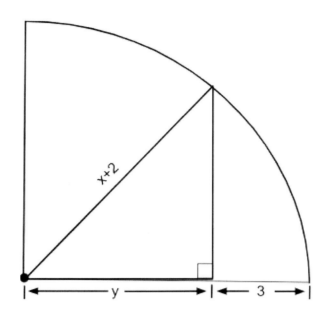

In the quarter circle above , what is y in terms of x?

    A) $x + 2$

    B) $x - 1$

    C) $\frac{x+2}{2}$

    D) $\sqrt{\frac{(x+2)}{2}}$

53. Jan walks into a man. Jan is $5'6''$, and the man is $184cm$. What is the difference between their heights, in centimeters? (Use $2.54cm = 1inch$)

  A) $21.12cm$

  B) $16.36\ cm$

  C) $19.23cm$

  D) $9.81cm$

54. What is the value of x in $4(7-3x) - (5-x) = 5x - 5$?

  A) $x = \frac{5}{2}$

  B) $x = \frac{10}{7}$

  C) $x = \frac{7}{4}$

  D) $x = 9$

55. Eric ate 3 less than triple as many candies as Henry did last week. If Eric ate 30 candies, how many did Henry eat last week?

  A) 11

  B) 12

  C) 13

  D) 14

SHSAT Mathematics Practice Test #8:

1. The height of a rectangular prism is ½ x, the width is ¼ x, and the length is ⅕ x. If x is equal to 20, what is the volume of this rectangular prism?

2. Evaluate:

$|-4|^3 - (-4) + \frac{1}{4} * 4 + 14$

3. $2^5 + 3^5 =$

4. What is the area of the figure below?

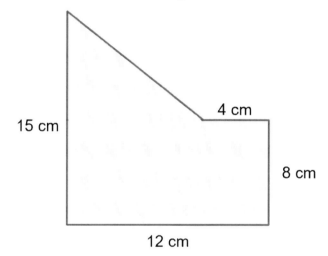

15 cm

4 cm

8 cm

12 cm

5. In the set of {41, 42, 43, 44...... 98,99, 100}, how many numbers are multiples of 6?

6. Perry left Adam's house and drove toward the ocean at an average speed of *42* mph. Adam left *2* hours later, driving towards the ocean with a speed of *70* mph. How long did Perry drive in total before Adam caught up?

   A) *7* hours

   B) *5* hours

   C) *4* hours

   D) *3* hours

7. In Frank's closet, there are 2 black hoodies, 4 white hoodies, 3 grey hoodies, and 1 red hoodie. What is the chance he does not choose a white hoodie?

   A) $\frac{6}{10}$

   B) $\frac{8}{10}$

   C) $\frac{2}{10}$

   D) $\frac{4}{10}$

8. What is the prime factorization of 56?

   A) $3^2 * 7$

   B) $3 * 7 * 9$

   C) $3^2 * 2 * 5$

   D) $2^3 * 7$

9. What is the value of x in $2(x + 5) + 5x = 4x + 1$?

   A) x = -3

   B) x = 7

   C) x = -9

   D) x = 5

10. There are 5 kids in the classroom who took a test. Two of the 5 kids got a 60 on it while the rest got a 100. What is the mean score of the test?

    A) 92

    B) 76

    C) 68

    D) 84

11. What is the value of the expression $|\frac{2}{3} - \frac{9}{6}| * 2\frac{9}{13}$?

    A) $\frac{35}{16}$

    B) $\frac{-35}{16}$

    C) $\frac{-175}{78}$

    D) $\frac{175}{78}$

12. The racetrack is 6 miles long. Ariana, a racer who is planning on racing around the race track, wants to complete the race track in 30 minutes. At what speed should Arianna drive to reach her goal?

    A) 12 miles per hour

    B) 6 miles per hour

    C) 3 miles per hour

    D) 9 miles per hour

13. If the pentagon below is a regular pentagon, what is the measure of a+b+c+d+e?

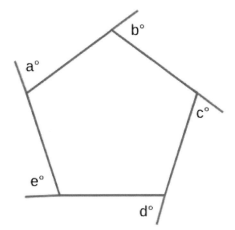

A) 180°

B) 270°

C) 360°

D) 540°

14. In a foreign country, the currency conversion rate is 1 bill = 30 coins. How many coins are equal to 48 bills?

A) 642 coins

B) 984 coins

C) 1440 coins

D) 1650 coins

15. If a = $\sqrt{96}$ and b = $\sqrt{48}$, what is $\frac{a}{b}$?

A) 0.5

B) 2

C) 4

D) $\sqrt{2}$

16. What is the value of the expression $\frac{3}{17} \div \frac{2}{5} * (\frac{24}{4} + \frac{5}{2})$?

    A) $\frac{30}{17}$

    B) $\frac{15}{4}$

    C) $\frac{47}{24}$

    D) $\frac{13}{9}$

17. Find the slope of the line that passes through the points (10,-4) and (-2, 8).

    A) 12

    B) -12

    C) 1

    D) -1

18. Ryan got paid $750 this week. If he bought a $100 gift for his brother and put 10% of the remaining amount into his savings account, how much money does Ryan now have?

    A) 565

    B) 575

    C) 585

    D) 595

19. What is x in terms of y?

$5(-3 + 2x) + 4x = y$

    A) $x = \frac{1}{14}y - \frac{15}{14}$

    B) $x = y + 15$

    C) $x = y - 15$

    D) $x = \frac{1}{14}y + \frac{15}{14}$

20. The product of two consecutive, even integers is 288. What is the greater number?

    A) 14

    B) 18

    C) 22

    D) 26

21. What is the difference between the exterior angle of an equilateral triangle and the exterior angle of a regular pentagon?

    A) 48

    B) 63

    C) 87

    D) 91

22. $\dfrac{5}{5n-4} = \dfrac{8}{n-3}$

    What is the value of n in the proportion above?

    A) $n = \dfrac{2}{5}$

    B) $n = \dfrac{3}{7}$

    C) $n = \dfrac{17}{35}$

    D) $n = \dfrac{14}{29}$

23. In the sequence [14, 15, 23, 13, 22, x] the mean of all the numbers is 18. What is the value of x?

    A) 23

    B) 18

    C) 21

    D) 17

24. $-6(x - 12) = 3x$

What is the value of x in the equation above?
- A) $x = 23$
- B) $x = 8$
- C) $x = 11$
- D) $x = 17$

25. What is the least common multiple of 20 and 56?

- A) 140
- B) 280
- C) 240
- D) 560

26. In the infinitely repeating decimal 0.1496314963, what will be the 33rd digit?

- A) 4
- B) 9
- C) 6
- D) 3

27. What is the area of the shape below?

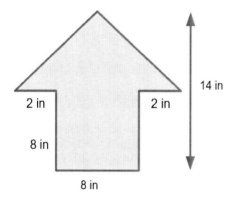

- A) 100 sq in
- B) 125 sq in
- C) 150 sq in
- D) 165 sq in

28. $4.3(b + 8.5) - 5.1(b - 9.9) = 86.88$

   What is the value of b in the above equation?
   A) $b = 2$
   B) $b = -3.2$
   C) $b = -11.9$
   D) $b = 0.2$

29.

Number of Siblings	Number of people
0	6
1	9
2	14
3 or more	1

   Jaden surveyed people around his neighborhood and recorded the number of siblings each person has. What is the chance of a person having at least 2 siblings?
   A) $\frac{16}{30}$
   B) $\frac{1}{30}$
   C) $\frac{1}{2}$
   D) $\frac{14}{30}$

30. Which of the following is equivalent to 6 less than the product of x and z?
   A) 6xz
   B) 6-xz
   C) xz-6
   D) xz+6

31. The equations of two lines are given below. At which point do these lines intersect?

$$0 = -12 + 12x - 24y$$

$$-7x + 4y = -27$$

   A) $(-5, 2)$

   B) $(5, -2)$

   C) $(5, 2)$

   D) $(-5, -2)$

32. When you write the integers from 3 to 60, how many times does a number with the digit 4 appear?

   A) 12

   B) 13

   C) 14

   D) 15

33. Solve the inequality

   $\frac{2x+5}{3} > 21$

   A) $x < 29$

   B) $x > 29$

   C) $x \leq 29$

   D) $x \geq 29$

34.

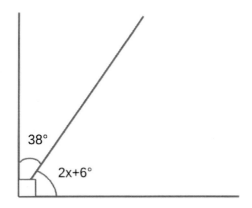

In the diagram above, what is the value of 2x?

A) 23

B) 31

C) 37

D) 46

35. A jar's capacity is 12 fluid ounces. How many liters can the jar hold? (Use $1L = 33.8 fl. oz$)

A) 0.36L

B) 2.42L

C) 1.92L

D) 0.93L

36. The lengths of the sides of a triangle are consecutive even numbers. What is the length of the shortest side if the perimeter is 90?

A) 27

B) 28

C) 29

D) 30

37. Which number set has the highest mode?

      A) [14,15,15,16,16,16,17,18,19,19]

      B) [15,15,15,15,17,17,18,19,19,20]

      C) [16,16,17,17,18,18,18,19,19,20]

      D) [16,16,16,16,21,21,23,24,25,28]

38. Exactly ⅙ of Sam's folders are green. Which of the following can be the total number of folders Sam owns?

      A) 7

      B) 16

      C) 52

      D) 84

39.

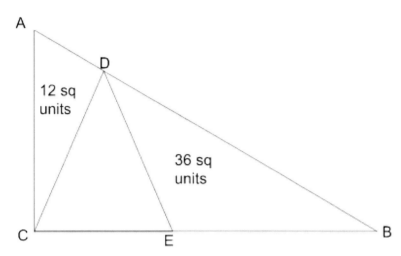

Triangle ABC, above, has an area of 70 sq units. What is the area of the triangle DCE?

      A) 48 sq units

      B) 22 sq units

      C) 24 sq units

      D) 35 sq units

40. Solve for x:

3(x-5)-5(2x-9) = 22

A) $\frac{7}{8}$

B) $\frac{8}{7}$

C) $-\frac{7}{8}$

D) $-\frac{8}{7}$

41. $\frac{8}{n+2} = -\frac{12}{7}$

What is the value of n in the equation above? (Round to the nearest hundredth)

A) $n = -6.67$
B) $n = -6.15$
C) $n = 11.24$
D) $n = 7.99$

42. A rectangular field is 30 yards wide and 10 yards long. If Pete runs 1 lap around the field at the speed of 10 yards per minute, how long, in minutes, does it take Pete to run?

A) 8 minutes

B) 4 minutes

C) 2 minutes

D) 16 minutes

43. Which of the following represents 625^2 in terms of a power of 5?

A) 5^8

B) 5^9

C) 5^{10}

D) 5^{11}

44. When $c(-4a - 2b) = 36$, what is the value of b in terms of a and c?

    A) $b = c + 2a$

    B) $b = -2c - 4a$

    C) $b = \frac{36}{c} + 4a$

    D) $b = -\frac{18}{c} - 2a$

45. In a rectangle, the length is 6 units and the width is triple the length of the rectangle. What is the perimeter of the rectangle?

    A) 18

    B) 48

    C) 54

    D) 108

46. Shawn walks at a pace of 9 miles every 4 hours, and Emma walks at a pace of 17 miles every 5 hours. What is the difference between their mileage if they both walked for 6 hours?

    A) 8.0

    B) 5.3

    C) 9.1

    D) 6.9

47. Which of the following is an inequality that represents half of a number minus five is less than five times the difference of 20 and the number?

    A) ½ x - 5 > 5(20-x)

    B) ½ x - 5 < 5(20-x)

    C) ½ x - 5 < 5(20+x)

    D) ½ x + 5 > 5(20-x)

48. If $x + 3 = 9$, what is the value of $5x + 7$?

    A) 7

    B) 17

    C) 37

    D) 27

49.

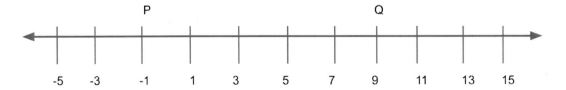

In the figure above, to what is the midpoint of PQ equal?

    A) 1

    B) 2

    C) 3

    D) 4

50. The heaviest package that a delivery company will ship weighs 150lbs. If a brick weighs 2 Kg, what is the maximum amount of bricks you can ship in a single package? (Use $1Kg = 2.2lb$)

    A) 34 bricks

    B) 49 bricks

    C) 28 bricks

    D) 51 bricks

51. The price of a sofa after a 40% discount is $360. What is the original price of the sofa?

    A) 380

    B) 420

    C) 480

    D) 600

52. What is the value of x if $x + 2 = \frac{4^2 - 3}{\sqrt{25}}$?

    A) $x = \frac{16}{25}$

    B) $x = \frac{3}{5}$

    C) $x = \frac{13}{5}$

    D) $x = \frac{13}{25}$

53. In a set of numbers from 1 to 200, how many numbers are divisible by 2 and 3?

    A) 30

    B) 31

    C) 32

    D) 33

54. If the area of a circle is 49π, what is the circumference of the circle?

    A) 7π

    B) 14π

    C) 21π

    D) 49π

55. $\frac{a-5}{a} = \frac{10}{8}$

    What is the value of a in the equation above?

    A) $a = -20$

    B) $a = -5$

    C) $a = -9$

    D) $a = -6$

SHSAT Mathematics Practice Test #9:

1. Morgan, Phil, Sarah, Joann, and Ed took a test. Morgan scored 72 points. Phil scored 69 points. Sarah scored 82 points. Joann scored 75 points. How many points did Ed score, if the mean score for the 5 tests is 76 points?

2. The sum of five consecutive, odd numbers is 495, what is the largest of the five integers?

3. A survey showed that 64% of people prefer buses over cars. If 90 people prefer cars over buses, what is the total number of people polled?

4. Johnny is twice Rose's weight. Mary is twice Johnny's weight. If, in total, they weigh 840 pounds, what is Johnny's weight?

5.

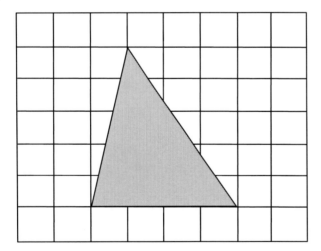

In the diagram above, each small box is a square with a side measuring 6 units. What is the area of the shaded figure?

6. The probability of picking a pink highlighter at random from a bag of 24 highlighters is ⅓. After, someone took out 3 pink highlighters and added 5 yellow highlighters. What is the chance of picking a pink highlighter?

   A) $\frac{5}{26}$

   B) $\frac{8}{26}$

   C) $\frac{11}{26}$

   D) $\frac{9}{26}$

7. What is the value of the expression $\frac{2}{5} * 3\frac{1}{2} - \frac{4}{3} / \frac{7}{3}$?

   A) $\frac{15}{24}$

   B) $\frac{7}{22}$

   C) $\frac{29}{35}$

   D) $\frac{-33}{24}$

8. What is the value of n in $\frac{2}{6} = \frac{\sqrt[3]{8}+n}{3}$?

   A) $n = \frac{1}{3}$

   B) $n = -1$

   C) $n = 0$

   D) $n = \frac{-2}{3}$

9. What is the solution to this system of equations?

$$x - \frac{5}{2}y = -\frac{3}{2}$$

$$10y + 4x = 14$$

A) $(1, -8)$

B) $(-8, -1)$

C) $(1,1)$

D) $(-8,1)$

10. The side of a cube is $5x^2$. What is the surface area of the cube?

A) $75x^2$

B) $75x^4$

C) $150x^2$

D) $150x^4$

11. What number could be the sum of five consecutive integers?

A) 52

B) 53

C) 54

D) 55

12. A plant grows at a rate of 86 centimeters in a year. What would be the plant's monthly growth rate in centimeters?

A) $4\frac{1}{2}$

B) $6\frac{5}{12}$

C) $7\frac{1}{6}$

D) $9\frac{3}{8}$

13. If $5x - 3y = 12$, what is the value of x?

    A) $x = \frac{3}{5}y + \frac{12}{5}$

    B) $x = -\frac{12}{5}y + \frac{3}{5}$

    C) $x = \frac{12}{5}y + \frac{3}{5}$

    D) $x = \frac{3}{5}y - \frac{12}{5}$

14. If a line passes through points A(-4,-2) and B(4,-4), what is its slope?

    A) 4

    B) $\frac{1}{4}$

    C) -4

    D) $-\frac{1}{4}$

15. What is the value of (3x+2y)(3x-y)?

    A) $9x^2 - 3xy - 2y^2$

    B) $9x^2 + 3xy - 2y^2$

    C) $9x^2 + 3xy + 2y^2$

    D) $- 9x^2 + 3xy - 2y^2$

16. {201,202,203,204......248,249,250}

In the set above, how many numbers of the set are multiple of 4?

    A) 10

    B) 11

    C) 12

    D) 13

17. What is the value of $\dfrac{9^{0.1\times 10^2}}{9^{100\times 10^{-2}}}$?

    A) 9^4

    B) 9^{-5}

    C) -9^3

    D) 9^9

18. A bowl has 3 pieces of frosted flakes, 8 pieces of marshmallows, and some pieces of circled cereal. The probability of choosing a marshmallow at random is twice as great as the probability of choosing a piece of a circled cereal at random. What is the probability that a piece of circled cereal will be chosen?

    A) $\dfrac{2}{15}$

    B) $\dfrac{3}{15}$

    C) $\dfrac{4}{15}$

    D) $\dfrac{5}{15}$

19. $|-3-4| + 4^2 * 12 - 8$

    A) 188

    B) 189

    C) 190

    D) 191

20. A garden wagon with a sack of cement in it weighs 86 pounds. It is being loaded with bricks they weigh 5 pounds. How many bricks can the truck load, if the maximum amount of weight the truck can hold is 345 pounds?

    A) 50 bricks

    B) 51 bricks

    C) 52 bricks

    D) 53 bricks

21.

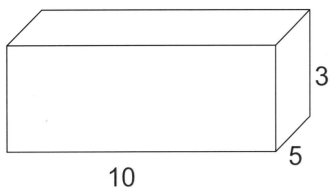

3

5

10

This box contains 2 tennis balls per cm^3 .How many tennis balls can the box fit?

    A) 300

    B) 150

    C) 15

    D) 30

22. The Verrazano bridge has a length of 4280 ft. A man is on the bridge in heavy traffic, driving at a constant speed of 7 km/h. How long will it take for the the man to cross the bridge, in minutes? (Use 1 meter $=$ 3.28 ft, round to the nearest hundredth)

    A) *18.74*

    B) *19.49*

    C) *14.24*

    D) *11.18*

23. A recipe to make a batch of paper mache recommends using a ratio of 4:5 cups of flour to cups of water. If Brad needs 117 cups of paper mache for one project, how much flour would he need if he wants to make 3 of these projects?

    A) 52 cups of flour

    B) 75 cups of flour

    C) 156 cups of flour

    D) 182 cups of flour

24. What is the value of 2a-3?

$$-2ab + 3b = 12$$

A) $\frac{2}{3}b$

B) $-\frac{12}{b}$

C) $\frac{3}{b} + 3$

D) $\frac{3}{2} - 6b$

25. What is 1000% of 5278?

A) 527.8

B) 5278

C) 52780

D) 527800

26. $2x = y$ and $y^6 = z$

If z equals to 64, what is x^4?

A) 1

B) 8

C) 16

D) 64

27. What is the value of b in terms of a in the equation below?

$$\sqrt{2b} = a - 3$$

A) $b = a^2 - 6a + 5$

B) $b = \frac{1}{2}a^2 - 3a + \frac{9}{2}$

C) $b = \frac{1}{3}a^2 + 2a - \frac{2}{3}$

D) $b = \frac{3}{4}a^2 - 5a + \frac{5}{2}$

28. If the width of a square pyramid is 8 inches and the height is 6 inches, what is the volume of the square pyramid?

    A) 21 cubic inches

    B) 36 cubic inches

    C) 81 cubic inches

    D) 128 cubic inches

29. The product of three consecutive numbers equals 720. What is the sum of the three consecutive numbers?

    A) 24

    B) 25

    C) 26

    D) 27

30. For what value of n does $-3(-5 - 2n) - 6(1 - 5n) = 9$?

    A) n = 9

    B) n = 18

    C) n = 0

    D) n = 2

31. $\dfrac{x-9}{x} = \dfrac{8}{3}$

    For what value of x is the equation above true?

    A) $x = -4.3$

    B) $x = 5.4$

    C) $x = -5.4$

    D) $x = 4.3$

32. The test scores of the class were recorded on the table below:

Student	*Scores*
Jimmy	78
Austina	93
Jerry	84
Katy	63
Robert	88
Jack	98

What is the difference between the mean score and Katy's score?

A) 31

B) 35

C) 25

D) 21

33. Find the value of t in the system of equations below.

$$2(s - 2t) = -20$$

$$4s + 3t = 4$$

A) 4

B) -3

C) 3

D) -4

34.

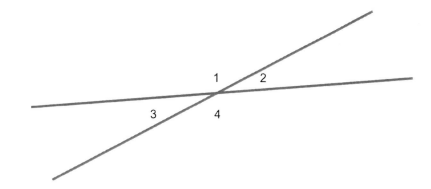

If angle 4 is 125°, what is the measure of angle 3?

A) 40

B) 55

C) 80

D) 135

35. For what value of n does $\frac{n+6}{2(2+7)} = \frac{6(n-9)}{3^3}$?

A) n = -14

B) n = 9

C) n = 24

D) n = 14

36. James has 5 different video games on top of his table. How many different ways can he arrange them?

A) 80

B) 100

C) 120

D) 140

37.

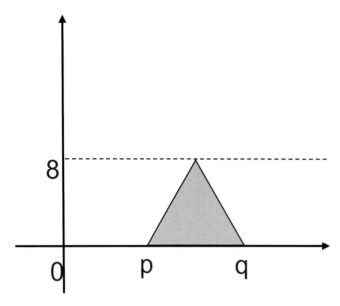

What is the area of the shaded triangle shown above?

A) $q - p$

B) $8(q - p)$

C) $4(p - q)$

D) $4(q - p)$

38. Chris, Aled, and Jonesy all go to a bakery. Chris buys 8 cupcakes and 5 muffins and pays \$23.75 in total. Aled buys 4 cupcakes and 11 muffins and pays \$35.35 in total. If Jonesy buys 3 cupcakes and 2 muffins, how much does he have to pay?

A) \$4.00

B) \$6.75

C) \$9.25

D) \$10.75

39. $\frac{m+11}{4} = -\frac{10}{6}$

What is the value of m? (Round to the nearest hundredth)

A) $m = -4.90$

B) $m = -17.67$

C) $m = -1.33$

D) $m = -12.25$

40. If an object was falling to the ground at a constant speed of 10 miles per hour, and the distance from the top to the bottom is ½ of a mile. How long will it take for the object to hit the ground?

A) 3 minutes

B) 5 minutes

C) 3 hours

D) 5 hours

41. The decimal 2.05 can be written as the fraction $\frac{a}{5}$. What is the value of a?

A) 6.75

B) 8.25

C) 10.25

D) 12.00

42. $106 = 3(6a + 6) + 5(9a + 5)$

For what value of a is the equation above true?

A) $a = 22$

B) $a = 1$

C) $a = -5$

D) $a = -19$

43. $\sqrt{324}$

    A) 18

    B) 19

    C) 16

    D) 17

44.   Below are the results of a survey asking people how many meals they ate every day. If 3,200 people were asked, how many more people eat 3 meals than people who eat 4 meals?

# of meals	Percentage
1	16%
2	24%
3	48%
4	12%

    A) 1,152

    B) 1,356

    C) 2,390

    D) 2,561

45. If $\frac{3}{4} = \frac{1}{12}x - \frac{3}{8}y$, what is y in terms of x?

    A) $-4 + \frac{4}{9}x = y$

    B) $\frac{2}{9}x - 2 = y$

    C) $\frac{1}{4}x - 5 = y$

D) $1 - \frac{1}{3}x = y$

46. On a coordinate plane, there are three points: A(-4,4), B(0,2), and C. If B is the midpoint of AC, what is the coordinate of point C?

    A) (2,0)

    B) (4,0)

    C) (0,4)

    D) (0,2)

47. If a is an integer, how many numbers could represent a if $7 \leq \sqrt{a} < 8$?

    A) 14

    B) 15

    C) 16

    D) 17

48. A beaker holds 572 mL of water. After a quarter of the water is poured out, how many quarts of water are left in the beaker? (Use 1 liter = 1.06 quarts, round to the nearest hundredth)

    A) *0.49 quart*

    B) *0.55 quart*

    C) *0.45 quart*

    D) *0.62 quart*

49. What is the value of $|5 - (3 - 4) - 10| - |6|$?

    A) -2

    B) 18

    C) 2

    D) -18

50. Lana tried to throw a ping pong ball into a basket 75 times. Out of those 75 times, only 20% of the time did the ping pong ball actually land in the basket. If Lana throws the ping pong ball 25 more times, what is the total predicted number of times the ball will land into the basket?

    A) 5
    B) 20
    C) 25
    D) 30

51. Which of the following inequalities represent this number line?

    A) $-3 \geq x \geq 7$
    B) $|3x - 6| > 15$
    C) $-3 \leq x \leq 7$
    D) $|3x - 6| < 15$

52. In a jar, there are 80 jellybeans. There are 32 blue jellybeans, 24 red jelly beans, 20 yellow jelly beans, and 4 pink jellybeans. What is the difference in the probability of drawing a blue jellybean compared to the probability of drawing a yellow jellybean?

    A) 10%
    B) 12%
    C) 15%
    D) 20%

53. What is the value of x in $7(5x - 4) - 1 = 12 - 6x$?

    A) x = 1

    B) x = -5

    C) x = 8

    D) x = 2

54. A bakery uses 32 bags of flour for 3,456 muffins. At the same rate, how many bags of flour are needed for 5,000 muffins?

    A) 46

    B) 47

    C) 48

    D) 49

55. Dean left the museum and started driving west. Jack left two hours later and drove 30 mph faster to try to catch up to Dean. He caught up with Dean 3 hours later. What was Dean's average speed?

    A) 45 mph

    B) 11 mph

    C) 15 mph

    D) 60 mph

SHSAT Mathematics Practice Test #10:

1.

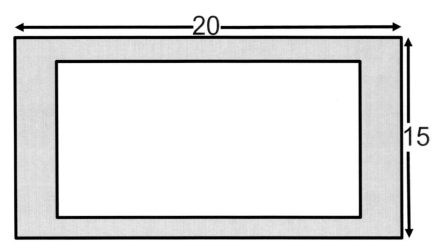

What is the area of the frame (shaded region) in the diagram above, if the inside picture has a width of 10 and a length of 5?

2. Jacob needs to organize 281 pounds of apples in a day. He needs to put 15 apples into the basket to fill the basket. He filled every basket except the last one. How many apples did he put in the last basket?

3. What is the greatest common factor of 192 and 144?

4. Based on the systems of equations below, what is the value of a?

$$5a - b = 12$$
$$6a + 3b = 6$$

5. How many terms are in the sequence: 0, 4, 8... 92, 96?

6. Which of the following numbers are divisible by 7 and 9?

    A) 28

    B) 98

    C) 108

    D) 252

7. What is the value of n in $-7n - 4(1 - 2n) = -4$?

    A) n = 2

    B) n = -2

    C) n = -7

    D) n = 0

8.

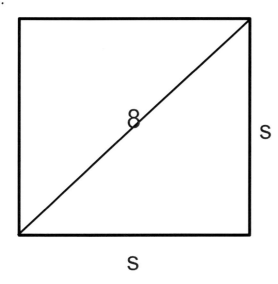

    What is the area of the square above, if the diagonals equal 8 units?

    A) $4\sqrt{2}$

    B) $\sqrt{16}$

    C) 32

    D) $\sqrt{32}$

9. x is the product of the reciprocal of ⅖ and the reciprocal of $\frac{4}{7}$. What is

   x^2 (rounded to the nearest tenth)?

   A) 0.1

   B) 18.1

   C) 19.1

   D) 20.1

10. Which of the following is a solution to the inequality below?

    7x + 4 > 52 + x

    A) 6

    B) 7

    C) 8

    D) 9

11. $4a + \frac{1}{2}b = 24$. What is 3a+1?

    A) $8 - \frac{5}{8}b$

    B) $-\frac{1}{8}b + 14$

    C) $19 - \frac{3}{8}b$

    D) $\frac{3}{8}b - 25$

12. Jessica left the hardware store and traveled toward the scrapyard. Two hours later, Jill left traveling at 75 km/h in an effort to catch up to Jessica. Having traveled for four hours, Jill finally caught up. What was Jessica's average speed?

    A) 70 km/h

    B) 60 km/h

    C) 50 km/h

    D) 55 km/h

13. When asked if they owned a vacuum cleaner in a survey, 88% of people answered yes. If 96 people did not answer yes, what is the total number of people who were given the survey?

    A) 800

    B) 1,152

    C) 6, 730

    D) 18,048

14. For what value of x does $2(\frac{1}{3} + \frac{2}{5}) + \frac{5}{4}x = \frac{3*154+1}{60}$?

    A) $x = 5$

    B) $x = \frac{2}{5}$

    C) $x = 1$

    D) $x = 2\frac{5}{2}$

15. $x^2 = y$ and $y^2 = z$. If z equals to 16, what does x^3 equal to?

    A) 12

    B) 4

    C) 6

    D) 8

16. In the set {10,11,12,13,....50,52,53,54}, how many numbers are divisible by 6?

    A) 6

    B) 7

    C) 8

    D) 9

17. What is the value of a^2 in $-2a + 4b = 16$?

    A) $2b - 8$

    B) $4b^2 - 4b + 16$

    C) $3b^2 + 16b - 48$

    D) $4b^2 - 32b + 64$

18. What is the volume of a cube with a side length of $\sqrt{3}$?

    A) $3\sqrt{3}$

    B) 3

    C) $2\sqrt{3}$

    D) 6

19. $4(x - 5.7) = -2.5(1 + 0.8x) + 3.1x$

What is the value of x in the equation above?

    A) $x = -7.6$

    B) $x = -6.4$

    C) $x = 13$

    D) $x = 7$

20. A driver's average speed is 45 mph. What is his average speed in feet per second?

    A) $59\ ft/sec$

    B) $66\ ft/sec$

    C) $62\ ft/sec$

    D) $86\ ft/sec$

21. What is the least common multiple of 28, 56, and 98?

    A) 196

    B) 392

    C) 280

    D) 980

22. Chris gets a weekly paycheck of $1,000. He wants to spend only $200 on food. If he spends $60 every time he goes grocery shopping, what is the greatest number of times he can go grocery shopping in a week?

    A) 1

    B) 2

    C) 3

    D) 4

23. $\dfrac{x-1}{7} = \dfrac{x}{8}$

What is the value of x in the proportion above?

    A) $x = 8$

    B) $x = 4$

    C) $x = 14$

    D) $x = 7$

24. If all the slices are identical, what is the area of the shaded portion?

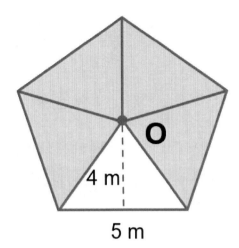

4 m

5 m

A) 20 sq m

B) 30 sq m

C) 40 sq m

D) 50 sq m

25. Alyssa has swimming lessons every 2 days. How many times will she go to swimming lessons if she goes there for 6 years straight?

A) 730 times

B) 1095 times

C) 2190 times

D) 3285 time

26. What is the solution to the system of equations below?

$$-7x - 8y = -1$$
$$21x + 24y = 6$$

A) $(9, -5)$

B) $(0,0)$

C) No solutions

D) Infinitely many solutions

27. Which one of these number sets has the highest median?

    A) [27,83,45,67,92]

    B) [12,12,53,56,99]

    C) [98,99,25,23,22]

    D) [109,87,52,13,28]

28. In a set of numbers from 0 to 40, how many numbers would have a 2 or 7 in them?

    A) 13

    B) 14

    C) 15

    D) 16

29.

On the number line above PQ = 7.55. What is the position of Point P?

    A) 11.9

    B) -11.9

    C) -3.2

    D) 3.2

30. A hot air balloon is continuously gaining altitude. Starting at 12:30PM, the hot air balloon continuously gains 475 feet per hour. If the hot air balloon started at 345 feet below sea level, what was the balloon's altitude above sea level at 5:30PM?

    A) 2750 ft

    B) 2030 ft

    C) 2375 ft

    D) 1900 ft

31. What is the value of x and y in the system of equations below?

$$6x - 2y = -12$$
$$-3x + 2y = 9$$

    A) $(-1,3)$

    B) $(3,-1)$

    C) $(-8,-1)$

    D) $(9,-1)$

32. $9(-4 - 15 \times 2) \times \frac{2}{36} =$

    A) -17

    B) 17

    C) 19

    D) -19

33. The sum of two consecutive integers is 35. What is the larger number divided by 6?

    A) 2

    B) 3

    C) 4

    D) 5

34. Which of the following points is closest to the origin?

   A) (5,8)

   B) (6,7)

   C) (-4,9)

   D) (7,7)

35.

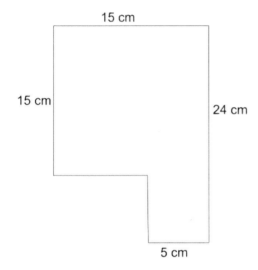

The figure above shows a scale drawing of a garden, where 1 centimeter represents 3 meters, what is the perimeter of the actual garden in meters?

   A) 150 meters

   B) 192 meters

   C) 162 meters

   D) 234 meters

36. Which of the following is a possible value of x in the inequality below?

$$30 > |3x - 9|$$

   A) -10

   B) -6

   C) 13

   D) 15

37. $\frac{n-10}{2} = \frac{n}{3}$

For what value of n is the proportion above true? (Round to the nearest tenth)

A) $n = 11.7$

B) $n = 11.6$

C) $n = -11.9$

D) $n = 30.0$

38. The distance between Asim's house and the grocery store is y, or $3x - 9$ miles west. The distance between the grocery store and his aunt's house is $\frac{1}{2}x + 4$ miles west. How long is the distance between Asim's house and his aunt's house, in terms of y?

A) $\frac{7y}{6} + \frac{11}{2}$ miles

B) $\frac{y}{6} + \frac{11}{2}$ miles

C) $\frac{y}{2} + 4$ miles

D) $2y + 6$ miles

39. A 6'2" American man is moving to Italy. For his I.D., the foreign ministry needs his height in centimeters. Find the man's height to the nearest centimeter. (Use 2.54 cm = 1in)

A) 148 cm

B) 154 cm

C) 179 cm

D) 188 cm

40. The mean of a number sequence is the same as its median, and its mode is 5. What is its mean value?

    A) 5

    B) 10

    C) Not enough information

    D) The same as the mode

41. The school has a total of 120 students, 66 of which are girls. What percent of the school is boys?

    A) 55 %

    B) 66%

    C) 50%

    D) 45%

42. What is the smallest prime number, x, such that ⅙ of x is greater than 15?

    A) 91

    B) 93

    C) 97

    D) 103

43. What is the value of x in $2(x + 17) - 8^2 = 3x$?

    A) x = 6

    B) x = -30

    C) x = 16

    D) x = -9

44. For what value of x is the proportion shown below true?

$$x : 49 = 3 : 7$$

   A) 10

   B) 21

   C) 3

   D) 7

45. A 12-foot long rectangular piece of metal has a proportionally shaped rectangular hole through it. If the sides of the piece of metal are twice as large as the sides of the hole, what is the total volume of the piece of metal? Assume the hole goes through the entire piece of metal.

6 feet

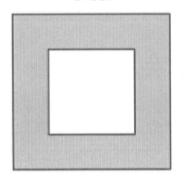

6 feet

   A) 108 cubic feet

   B) 256 cubic feet

   C) 324 cubic feet

   D) 432 cubic feet

46. The temperature of a pan is 203 F°. Every hour, the pan's temperature decreases by 5 C°. How long will it take for the pan to reach 20 C°? Round to the nearest tenth place. Use the formula, $(F - 32)\frac{5}{9} = C$.

   A) 9 hours

   B) 12 hours

   C) 15 hours

   D) 18 hours

47.

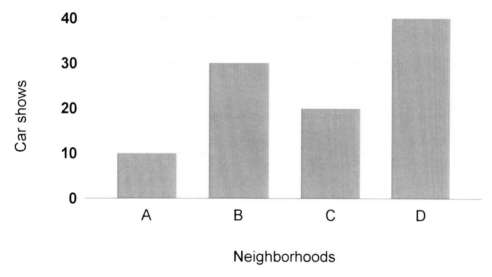

Number of car shows in the neighborhood

The graph above shows the number of car shows per neighborhood in 4 big neighborhoods. Neighborhoods A and B have 300 cars per car show. Neighborhood C has 400 cars per car show. Neighborhood D has 100 cars per car show. Which of the four neighborhoods has the greatest number of cars?

   A) Neighborhood A

   B) Neighborhood B

   C) Neighborhood C

   D) Neighborhood D

48. A password of 7 digits is made up of 9220338. How many possible passwords are there?

    A) 1070

    B) 1120

    C) 1260

    D) 1480

49. $\left(\frac{12^3 \times 12^4}{4^7}\right)$

Simplify the expression above.

    A) 1895

    B) 2187

    C) 2249

    D) 2317

50. Glenn is running at a rate of 6.5 miles per hour. Lola is 9 miles behind Glenn. If Lola runs at a rate of 8 miles per hour, how long will it take her to catch up to Glenn?

    A) 1 hour

    B) 3 hours

    C) 6 hours

    D) 7 hours

51. Find an equation of the line that has a slope of 3 and passes through the point (2,8).

    A) y= 3x + 2

    B) y= 3x

    C) y= -3x -2

    D) y = 3x - 2

52. X is the reciprocal of $-\frac{4}{7}$. What does 2x + 5 equal?

    A) -1.5

    B) 1.5

    C) 2

    D) 2.5

53. What is the value of x in $-4 - 4(-x - 1) = -4(6 + 2x)$?

    A) x = 2

    B) x = -3

    C) x = 5

    D) x = -2

54. If lines $\underline{WX}$ and $\underline{YZ}$ are parallel to each other, what is the measure of angle x?

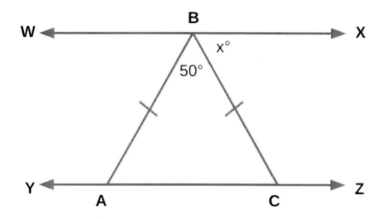

    A) 50°

    B) 65°

    C) 75°

    D) 130°

55. Shelly purchased two ropes that were 40 meters and 200 centimeters, respectively. Jenny also purchased two ropes, that were 16 meters and 370 centimeters, respectively. What is the total length of the four ropes, in feet? (Use 1 m = 3.28 ft, round to the nearest hundredth)

    A) 202.43 ft

    B) 209.84 ft

    C) 202.38 ft

    D) 209.11 ft

Practice Test #1 Answers:

1. **Answer: 2**

   Expand $x^2 + 6x - 16$ into $(x - 2)(x + 8)$. Then, you set the two expressions equal to 0. $x - 2 = 0$ only when x equals 2, and $x + 8 = 0$ when x equals -8. 2 is the only positive value that makes the equation true.

2. **Answer: 41**

   Triangle ABC is a right triangle. We know that angle CAE is 45 degrees and ABC is 90 degrees, which makes angle ACB equal to 45. The exterior angle of angle DCB is 105 degrees. Since angle ACB is a part of DCB, we can use what we know to find what angle ECD is: a + 45 = 75 (75 is the interior angle), or a = 30. Angle ECD is equal to 30.

   Now, we can find the measure of angle AEB: 45 + 26 + b = 180 or b = 109. Because angle AEB is a vertical angle to angle DEC, they are equivalent. Angle DEC=109.

   Now that we know that angle DEC=109 and ECD=30, we can find x:

   109 + 30 + x = 180, or x = 41.

3. **Answer: 2.25**

   We can convert $\frac{6}{16}$ to $\frac{3}{8}$ to make addition easier:

   Add: $\frac{3}{8} + \frac{5}{8} = 1$

   Convert the fractions to decimals: $\frac{1}{2} + \frac{3}{4} = 0.5 + 0.75 = 1.25$

   Add together: 1.25 + 1 = 2.25

4. **Answer: 28.3**

   The formula for the area of a circle is A $=r^2\pi$. Divide the diameter by 2 to get the radius of the circle: $6 \div 2 = 3$. $3^2\pi = 28.26$, which is 28.3 when rounded to the nearest tenth.

5. **Answer: 2**

   When adding the two equations, you will get $15x = 30$. Then, divide both sides of the equations by 15 to isolate the variable. Once that is done you get $x = 2$ as your answer.

6. **Answer: D**

   1) $\frac{-37}{10} \div \frac{9}{4}$ *Rewrite mixed numbers as improper fractions*

   2) $\frac{-37}{10} * \frac{4}{9}$ *Divide fractions by multiplying by the reciprocal of the second fraction*

   $\frac{-37*4}{10*9}$

   $\frac{-148}{90}$

   3) $\frac{-148 \div 2}{90 \div 2}$ *Simplify using greatest common factor (GCF = 34)*

   $\frac{-74}{45}$ *Final answer.*

7. **Answer: B**

   There are 12 inches in one foot, so we would multiply 5 and 12 inches together in order to convert feet to inches, which would get you 60 inches. We add the 8 inches to the 60 in order to find the total amount of inches that need to be converted into centimeters, which gets you 68 inches. In order to convert our inches to centimeters, we multiply 68 inches by 2.54 centimeters, and we get our answer of 172.72 centimeters.

8. **Answer: C**

   The factors of 117 are 1, 3, 9, 13, 39, and 117. The numbers that are prime numbers are 3 and 13 since their only factors are the number itself and 1. Since 13 is greater than 3, 13 is the answer.

9. **Answer: C**

   When multiplying your new product keeps factors of the previous number. For example, when multiplying 3 and 2 together your product, 6, has the same factors as its multiplicands, 3 and 2. However, when adding your sum does not keep the factors, unless you add a number that shares a factor with the other addend. As $5p + 9$ is the only expression with an addend that is a multiple of 3, C is the answer.

10. **Answer: B**

    First, we subtract $60.50 from $50 to find the amount of money Daria paid for the miles she drove, 60.50 - 50= 10.50. Then, divide $10.50 by $0.35 to find the number of miles Daria paid for, $10.50 \div 0.35 = 30$. Since the first 15 miles were free, we add 15 to 30 to find the total number of miles Daria drove, $15 + 30 = 45$, which is 45 miles.

11. **Answer: A**

    First, subtract $\frac{4}{3}$ from both sides of the equation to isolate the variable, to get $\frac{x-8}{6} = \frac{-1}{3}$. After this we cross-multiply, resulting in $-6 = 3x - 24$. To further isolate the variable, we add 24 to both sides of the equation to get $18 = 3x$. Then, divide both sides of the equation by 3, to get the final answer of $6 = x$.

12. **Answer: B**

The formula the volume of a cylinder is $h\pi r^2$. Area= πr^2, which when substituted with the information we know we can replace it with 36π square inches. However, the units of the height is in feet, so we convert square inches to square inches by dividing by 144, resulting in 0.25π square feet. Our formula now looks like $6 * 0.25 * \pi$ or $6 * 0.25 * 3.14$, which results in 4.71 cubic feet.

13. **Answer: A**

In order to solve this problem, set up the equation, $\frac{6}{x} = \frac{3}{8}$. Cross multiply to get the equation $3x = 48$. Then, isolate the variable by dividing by 3 on both sides, which equals 6 cards. x in our equation equals the total amount of cards, and we are trying to find the number of cards that are not green, subtract 6 from the total amount to get 10 not green cards.

14. **Answer: C**

1) 686: 2, 7, 7, 7
   1862: 2, 7, 7, 19   *Find prime factors of numerator and denominator*

2) 2,7,7   *List all common factors*

3) 2 * 7 * 7 = 98   *Multiply factors. This is the greatest common factor*

4) $\frac{686 \div 98}{1862 \div 98}$ *Divide the numerator & denominator by the GCF*

$\frac{7}{19}$ *Final answer*

15. **Answer: D**

To isolate the variable, subtract 20 from both sides and divide by 60 on both sides of the inequality. The inequality is now x ≤ 5, and 5 is equal to 5.

16. **Answer: C**

To isolate x add 14y to both sides of the equation, 10x = 17y, and divide both sides by 10 to get $x = \frac{17}{10} + \frac{7}{5}y$.

17. **Answer: C**

We can first factor both 72 and 30:

30 factors: 1, 2, 3, 5, 6, 10, 15, 30

72 factors: 1, 2, 3, 4, 6, 8, 9, 12, 18, 24, 36, 72

From this, we can find the greatest common factor, which is 6. Meaning that the stick is 6 ft. long.

18. **Answer: B**

Isolate x:

Distribute -3 into the inequality: $|-12x - 6| \leq 30$

Solve for the absolute value by breaking the inequality into two inequalities,

$-12x - 6 \leq 30$ and $-12x - 6 \leq -30$:

Solve: $-12x - 6 \leq 30$

Add 6 on both sides: $-12x \leq 36$

Divide by -12: $x \geq -3$

(we switch the signs because we are dividing with a negative number)

Solve: $-12x - 6 \geq -30$

Add 6 on both sides: $-12x \geq -24$

Divide by -12: $x \leq 2$

(we switch the signs because we are dividing with a negative number)

Combine the two inequality solutions into one inequality to get $-3 \leq x \leq 2$ as your final answer.

19. **Answer: C**

The two consecutive integers whose sum will equal 23 are 11 and 12. Since 11 is less than 12 you have to add 3 to it and subtract 5 from 12: *11 + 3 = 14* and *12 − 5 = 7*. Then, find product of 14 and 7 to get 98 as your final answer.

20. **Answer: A**

The sum of two opposite interior angles (Angle ABC and angle BAC) is equal to the exterior angle.

Use this equation to find angle BCA:

$(3x + 4) + (4x − 4) = 6x + 20 \rightarrow$ x=20.

Now that we know what x is equal to, find the measure of angle BCD: (20)+20=140.

Now, subtract by 180 to get your final answer, since angle BCD is the supplementary angle of angle BCA:

180-140=40

21. **Answer: B**

Solve for x by multiplying both sides of the equation by 3 and then subtracting from both sides of the equation, which results in $−4x = 24$. Finally, divide by -4 from both sides of the equation to isolate x, which results in x = -6.

22. **Answer: B**

Simplify both the radicals first, if possible:

$8\sqrt{6}$ can't be simplified further.

$4\sqrt{48}$ can be simplified to $4 \times \sqrt{16} \times \sqrt{3}$ which is equal to $4 \times 4 \times \sqrt{3}$. The expression in simplest form is $8\sqrt{6} − 16\sqrt{3}$.

23. Answer: D

$\frac{3}{5}$ of the total are boys; thus, $1 - \frac{3}{5} = \frac{2}{5}$ of the total are girls.

$\frac{2}{5}$ of 600 students is 240 students.

Of these 240 students, $\frac{1}{3}$ are in 6th grade. $\frac{1}{3}$ of 240 is 80 students.

Thus, 80 students in the auditorium are 6th grade girls.

24. Answer: A

After using the inverse operation to get the variable on just one side, multiply both sides by 5 to get $4x^2 = 100$. Continue using the inverse operations, and divide both sides by 4, which gives us $x^2 = 25$. Finally, solve for x by squaring both sides, which gives you 5 in this case.

25. Answer: C

First, we find Betty's rate at meters per minute by multiplying her rate by 60, since there are 60 seconds in one minute:

$\frac{4}{1} * \frac{60}{60}$, or $\frac{240}{60}$. This means Betty can run 240 meters per minute.

Then, find how many kilometers she runs each minute by multiplying her rate by 0.001, since there are 0.001 kilometers, to get a rate of 0.24 meters per minute. Finally, we divide the length of the race by the number of meters in a minute Betty can run:

$5 \div 0.24 = 20.83$ or 20.83 minutes, once rounded to the nearest hundredth place.

26. Answer: B

First, find the factors of 91 and 98:

The factors of 91 are 1,7,13,91.

The factors of 98 are 1,2,7,14,48 and 98.

As you can see, the greatest number they have in common is 7.

27. **Answer: B**

The formula for the volume of a rectangular prism is $width * length * height$. The volume of the holes is 180 cubic feet because it takes 180 cubic feet of cement to fill the hole.

Since you know the width (5 feet) and the length (12 feet), replace them with the variables in the formula: $5 * 12 * height = 180 \rightarrow 60 * height = 180$.

We then can divide 60 on both sides of the equation to isolate the variable, the height, to get $height = 3$, meaning that the depth of the hole is 3 feet.

28. **Answer: A**

Set up the equation as $x + (2x - 15) = 180$. Then, combine like terms to get the new equation of $3x - 15 = 180$. To isolate the variable, add 15 to both sides of the equation and divide by 3 on both sides of the equation to get that x equals 65. To find angle A, subtract 15 from x to get 50.

29. **Answer: B**

There are 55 other chocolates besides dark chocolate, which means that 55 would be the numerator. There are 80 total chocolates so 80 would be the denominator, making the answer $\frac{55}{80}$ or $\frac{11}{16}$ when simplified.

30. **Answer: C**

$5^x = \sqrt{625}$. When 625 is square rooted you get 25 and a new equation of $5^x = 25$ Therefore, x = 2 since you know that 5 squared equals 25.

31. **Answer: C**

The percentage of people who like blue and black are $\frac{65}{100}$. The percent of people who like green and red are $\frac{11}{100} + \frac{24}{100} = \frac{35}{100}$. Subtract the two to find how much greater the percentage of people who like black and blue is than the percentage of people who like green and red$\frac{65}{100} - \frac{35}{100} = \frac{30}{100}$

32. **Answer: A**

These are the formulas that need to be used: $x = \frac{p}{r}, s = \frac{t}{g}$

1) $(\frac{p}{r})/(\frac{t}{g})$ *Plug in variables with the information in the question*

2) $\frac{p}{r} * \frac{g}{t}$ *Divide fractions by multiplying by the reciprocal*

$\frac{p*g}{r*t}$ *Multiply numerators and denominators to get one fraction*

$\frac{pg}{rt}$ *Final answer*

33. **Answer: D**

Assuming r= the radius and h = the height, the formula of the volume of a cylinder is $r^2\pi h$. Replacing the variables with the given values, we would have: $6^2\pi 4$. Since we are using π=3.14, the equation would then look like: $6^2 * 3.14 * 4$ to get 452.16 cubic inches. To find one slice of the cake, which is cut into 8ths, find the volume by $\frac{1}{8}*$452.16 to get 56.52 cubic inches.

34. **Answer: C**

x will equal any of the heights of the trees on the farm. x must be greater than or equal to 24, because 24 is the smallest possible height. x must be less than or equal to 31, because 31 is the largest possible height. When you put that information into one inequality, you get $24 \le x \le 31$.

35. **Answer: B**

To solve this problem, we need to cross multiply $\frac{6}{5x-5} = \frac{3}{5}$ to get an equation of $30 = 3(5x - 5)$. Next, distribute 3 into $(5x - 5)$: $15x - 15$.

Our equation is now $30 = 15x - 15$. To isolate x, add 15 to both sides of the equation to get $45 = 15x$. Then, to isolate further divide both sides of the equation by 15 to get x= 3.

36. **Answer: D**

First, let's find how many cookies Sharon makes in terms of x. She makes four less than 3 times the amount Marie makes, which when represented by an expression is $3x - 4$.

We know Benson makes half the amount Sharon makes, so divide 3x-4 by 2:

$$\frac{3x - 4}{2}$$

Now, we can simplify by dividing by 2: $\frac{3x}{2} - \frac{4}{2} \rightarrow \frac{3x}{2} - 2$

Our answer is D, because $-2 + \frac{3x}{2}$ is equivalent to $\frac{3x}{2} - 2$, the only difference is that the order of the numbers was changed.

37. **Answer: D**

A common denominator that $\frac{1}{2}$, ¾ , and $\frac{7}{8}$ have is 16. The denominators of these mixed fractions as 16 look like $2\frac{8}{16}$, $5\frac{12}{16}$, and $1\frac{14}{16}$. Turn the mixed fractions into improper fractions: $\frac{40}{16}$, $\frac{92}{16}$, and $\frac{30}{16}$, respectively. Add all the numerators together to get a sum of 162.

38. **Answer: C**

We can set up a system of equations to help us solve this problem (assume s is the number of sailboats and t is the number of tugboats):

$$s + t = 10$$

$$45s + 12t = 252$$

Find the number of tugboats by finding s is in terms of t, so isolate s in the equation $s + t = 10$ to get 10-t=s.

Then, we can replace s in the second equation:

$45(10 - t) + 12t = 252.$

Solve for t:

Multiply 45: $450 - 45t + 12t = 252.$

Simplify: $450 - 33t = 252.$

Subtract 450 on each side : $-33t = -198.$

Divide -33 on each side: t=6

This means there are 6 tugboats. Then, we find the number of sailboats by plugging t into the first equation: subtract 6 from the total number of boats and you get 4.

39. **Answer: A**

First, we must find the slope of the line AB. Using the slope formula, $\frac{y2-y1}{x2-x1}$, we would get $\frac{-3-(-1)}{-3-3} = \frac{1}{3}$. Because the line is parallel, the slope would be the same.

40. **Answer: A**

$63 \div 16 = 3.93.$ The question is asking for how many 16-student groups can be made, so round down to 3 since you can't have part of a student in one group.

41. **Answer: D**

    First, we need to find the rate of the number of pages Maria reads per hour. There are 60 minutes in an hour, and Maria takes 30 minutes to read 6 pages, which means that it would take Maria an hour to read 12 pages. Now, divide 216 by 12 in order to find the total amount of time it takes for her to read the entire book, 18 hours.

42. **Answer: B**

    We want to isolate x by adding 6 to both sides of the equation. As a result, the equation is $3h^3 = 192$. Next, divide both sides of the equation by 3 to get the new equation of $h^3 = 64$. Finally, find the cube root of 64, which is 4.

43. **Answer: C**

    First, we need to find out what the temperature will be at 6 P.M. in Fahrenheit. Since the temperature rises 2°F every hour and the time elapsed is 7 hours, we end up with an increase of 14°F. We add that to the original 66°F and get a result of 80°F. Now, we plug 80°F into the formula given, $(F - 32) \times \frac{5}{9} = C$, and we end up with a final answer of 26.7°F

44. **Answer: D**

    Cross-multiply the proportion to get 3(x+8)=2(2x+6). Using the distributive property of multiplication, simplify both sides of the equation, meaning that 3(x+8) becomes 3x+24, and 2(2x+6) becomes 4x+12 and together that makes 3x+24=4x+12. We can then isolate the variable by subtracting 3x and 12 from both sides of the equation to get a new equation of 12=x.

45. **Answer: A**

First, we must square both sides of the equation to get a new equation of $4x = 64$.

To isolate x, divide both sides of the equation by 4, to get $x = 16$.

46. **Answer: B**

Set up the proportion as $\frac{8}{y} = \frac{136}{68}$. Cross multiply 8 and 68 and then set it equal to 136 times y, 544 = 136y. To solve for y, isolate the variable by dividing both sides of the equation by 136 to get y= 4.

47. **Answer: B**

Mean is found by adding up all the numbers and then dividing that sum by the total number of addends:

$$24 + 45 + 3 + 28 = 100$$
$$1 \quad 2 \quad 3 \quad 4$$
$$100 \div 4 = 25$$

48. **Answer: D**

We first have to find out how many questions Brent and Larry can solve individually. There are 60 minutes in an hour.

If Brent can solve 5 questions in 6 minutes, in order to find how many questions he can solve in 60 minutes, multiply 6 and 5 by 10, which tells us he can solve 50 questions in 60 minutes.

If Larry can solve 10 questions in ten minutes, he can solve 60 questions in 60 minutes.

Add them together and get 110 questions in total.

49. **Answer: A**

First, distribute the -1:

Distribute: 4x − 3 − 2 − 3x − 5 = y

Combine like terms: x − 10 = y

Isolate x: x = y + 10

50. **Answer: C**

Since there are 60 seconds in a minute and 60 minutes in an hour, there are 3,600 seconds in an hour. If there are four hours, then there will be 14,400 seconds. 20 minutes in seconds will be *20 ∗ 60* which is equal to 1200. *14,400 + 1,200* is equal to 15,600.

51. **Answer: A**

The word problem can be expressed as *4x − 2 = 5x + 12*. Variables and constants need to be put on opposite sides by subtracting 4x from both sides of the equation to get *−2 = x + 12* and subtracting 12 from both sides of the equation to get -14 = x.

52. **Answer: D**

8.625 as a improper fraction would be $\frac{69}{8}$, and 3.75 as a improper fraction would be $\frac{30}{8}$. Now, subtract the two together: $\frac{69}{8} - \frac{30}{8} = \frac{39}{8}$.

53. **Answer: A**

The statement "product of 7 and y" illustrates that 7 and y are multiplied together. "40 added" indicates the operation done will be addition. "Exceeds" means that the inequality sign has to be greater than sign.

54. **Answer: B**

By using the rules of exponents: whenever an exponent is put to the power of another exponent you multiply them. In this case, $\frac{5}{7}$ x -2 = $-\frac{10}{7}$. $14^{-\frac{10}{7}}$ is the same as $14^{-1} \times 14^{-\frac{3}{7}}$.

55. **Answer: D**

First, we need to find the rate of the number of miles traveled in 1 hour. We can do this by simplifying our rate, $\frac{180}{6}$ or $\frac{30}{1}$, meaning in 1 hour, the train travels 30 miles.

Then, subtract 180 from 1,560 because we need to find how much longer it will take to Point B, which is 1,380 miles. This is because the 180 miles already traveled is not included in our answer.

We then divide 1,380 by 30, and we get 46 hours.

Practice Test #2 Answers:

1. **Answer: 0.48**

   1) $177 + 12 + 7 + 4 = 200$ *Find total of ratio*

   2) $12 : 200$ *Ratio of zinc to coin*

       $x : 8$ *Ratio of mass of zinc to mass of coin*

   3) $\frac{12}{200} = \frac{x}{8}$ *Ratios equivalent to each other*

       $200x = 12 * 8$

       $200x = 96$ *Cross-multiplication*

   4) $x = \frac{96}{200}$ *Isolate variable*

       $x = \frac{96 \div 2}{200 \div 2}$

       $x = \frac{48}{100}$ *Set denominator equal to 100*

   5) $\frac{48}{100} = 0.48$

       $x = 0.48$ *Convert fraction to decimal*

       $0.48 \ g$ *Final answer*

2. **Answer: 3**

   First we can simplify both sides of the equation. On the left side, 7^2 gives us 49. On the right side, $19 * 2^2 = 19 * 4 = 76$. This gives us the equation of $x^3 + 49 = 76$. We then subtract 49 from both sides of the equation, giving us $x^3 = 27$. Taking the cube root of both sides of the equation gives us our final answer of $x = 3$.

3. **Answer: 120**

   Since order doesn't matter, it's a combination. Combination can be calculated with x! Where x represents the number of items you have. In this problem, x is equal to 5 and $5! = 5 \times 4 \times 3 \times 2 \times 1 = 120$.

4. **Answer: 16**

   Find the distance the freight train traveled before catching up with the diesel train

   1) $40km/h * 10\ hours = 400km$ *Speed * Time = Distance*

   Find the time the diesel train traveled before being caught up with.

   2) $25km/h * x\ hours = 400km$ *Plug in distance*

   3) $25x = 400$ *Solve for x*

   $x = 16\ hours$

5. **Answer: 84**

The surface area is the total area of the outside of the shape. A square pyramid has 5 faces, 4 are identical triangles and a square base.

Here, we can find the area of the face, using the formula to find the area of a triangle, $\frac{base * height}{2}$, or $\frac{6 * 4}{2}$ once we have replaced the given values into the formula. Simplify and we get 12 square yards, the area of the face. Then multiply by 4, because there are 4 identical triangle faces in a square pyramid, giving us 48 square yards. We then find the area of the square base, which is 6*6, or 36. We then add the two values together, 48+36, or 84 square yards.

6. **Answer: C**

We can set up an equation for proportion which would be $\frac{.6}{10} = \frac{x}{80}$ and solve for x. Next, you cross multiply 80 and .6 along with 10 and x to get the equation 48 = 10x and then solve for x which is 4.8.

7. **Answer: B**

Set up the expression x + 4x = 90 Combine like terms and you should get 5x = 90. Then, divide 5 on both sides of the equation to get x = 18.

8. **Answer: B**

We first must factor the number 91. This gives us the prime factorization of $7 * 13$, the smallest factor being 7. Next, looking through the answer choices, the only answer that is a multiple of 7 (i.e., has 7 as a factor) is 35. Thus, our answer is 35.

9. **Answer: D**

In order to find the value of x in terms of y, we need to isolate a:

Subtract $\frac{9}{4}$ from both sides: $a^3 = 3b^2 - \frac{9}{4}$

Find the cubed root on both sides: $a = \sqrt[3]{3b^2 - \frac{9}{4}}$

10. **Answer: C**

The volume of a right pyramid can be expressed as $V = \frac{lwh}{3}$. Since the base is a square, the length and width will be 4. Once we plug it into the equation, the equation will now be $V = \frac{(16)(10)}{3}$. As a result, V is equal to 53.333, which rounds to 53 cubic feet.

11. **Answer: B**

We can set up a system of equations that can help us solve this problem. Assume q= the number of quarters and d=the number of dimes.

$$q + d = 50$$

$$0.25q + 0.10d = 10.25$$

Now, we can solve. Because we are trying to find the number of d (d), we can isolate q in equation $q + d = 50$ to find the value of q in terms of d, giving us $q = 50 - d$. We can replace q in equation $0.25q + 0.10d = 10.25$, or $0.25(50 - d) + 0.10d = 10.25$. Distribute 0.25, and we get $12.5 - 0.25d + 0.10d = 10.25$. We can then simplify, $12.5 - 0.15d = 10.25$. Subtract 12.5 on each side and we get, $-0.15d = -2.25$. We divide -0.15 on each side and we get 15. This is the amount of dimes in the piggy bank.

12. **Answer: C**

We can set up a permutation of $_7P_3$, which would be $\frac{7!}{(7-3)!}$. This results in, $\frac{7!}{4!}$, which can be written as 7*6*5. This results in an answer of 210.

13. **Answer: A**

We want to find Mei's rate at $\frac{8\ pages}{x\ hour}$. We know Mei's rate is $\frac{3\ pages}{5\ hours}$, so we can cross multiply the two rates to find x, the number of hours Mei takes to write 8 pages. We get x=$13\frac{1}{3}$, meaning Mei takes $13\frac{1}{3}$ hours to write 8 pages.

Finally, we subtract $13\frac{1}{3}$ and 5, because we are finding the remaining hours it takes Mei to write her pages, giving us $8\frac{1}{3}\ hours$.

14. **Answer: A**

Distribute the -1: $2x + 6 - 3x + 4$

Combine like terms: $-x + 10$

15. **Answer: C**

1) $50\% = \frac{50}{100} = \frac{1}{2}$ *Convert percentage to fraction*

2) $\frac{1}{2} * \frac{15}{10}$ *Multiply fractions*

$\frac{1*15}{2*10}$ *Multiply numerators and denominators*

$\frac{15}{20}$

3) $\frac{15*5}{20*5}$ *Set denominator equal to 100*

$\frac{75}{100}$

4) $\frac{75}{100} = 0.75$ *Convert fraction to decimal*

0.75 *Final answer*

16. **Answer: D**

The starting amount that Mark has is 100; therefore, it doesn't need a variable. Since he earns 15 an hour, there needs to be a variable next to it since it is constantly increasing. The > sign needs to be used since we need to know the least number of hours he needs to work.

17. **Answer: D**

The even factors of 180 that are greater than 10 and less than 60 include 12,18,20,30,36,45.

18. **Answer: B**

We know side AB is 12. And we know that all sides are equal in squares. That means that side DC is also 12 and the midpoint of side DC is E. We know that the midpoint cuts the line in half. So side DE equals 12 / 2 = 6. Knowing side DE= 6 and knowing side AD = 12 we can find the area using the area of triangle formula $(\frac{1}{2} Base \ x \ Height)$.

Plug in the values   > $\frac{1}{2}6 \ x \ 12$

Solve   >   3 x 12 = 36

19. **Answer: D**

1) $\frac{2}{3}(\frac{9}{5} * \frac{13}{9}) + \frac{1}{2}$ *Divide fractions: Multiply by reciprocal*

2) $\frac{2}{3}(\frac{9*13}{5*9}) + \frac{1}{2}$

$\frac{2}{3}(\frac{117}{45}) + \frac{1}{2}$ *Multiply numerators and denominators*

3) $\frac{2*117}{3*45} + \frac{1}{2}$

$\frac{234}{135} + \frac{1}{2}$ *Multiply numerators and denominators*

4) $\frac{234*2}{135*2} + \frac{1*135}{2*135}$

$\frac{468}{270} + \frac{135}{270}$ *Add fractions using common denominator (LCM 270)*

5) $\frac{468+135}{270}$ *Add numerators*

6) $\frac{603}{270}$

$\frac{603÷9}{270÷9}$ *Simplify using greatest common factor (GCF = 9)*

7) $\frac{67}{30}$ *Final answer.*

20. **Answer: B**

Plug every value of the set into the equation to find all possible values of b. 3(4) + 1 = 13. 6(3) + 1 = 19. 8(3) + 1 = 25. 9(3) + 1 = 28. 11(3) + 1 = 34.

13, 19, 25, 28, and 34 are values in b.

21. **Answer: C**

There are 5280 feet in a mile and there are 3,600 seconds in an hour.

If we multiply 6 by 5280, we get 31,680.

We then divide 31,680 by 3,600 and we receive a rate of 8.8 feet per second.

22. **Answer: A**

We can write this proportion in fraction form: $\frac{16}{28} = \frac{x}{42}$. We can first simplify $\frac{16}{28}$ into $\frac{4}{7}$. Now with our new proportion, $\frac{4}{7} = \frac{x}{42}$, we can solve for x.

$7x = 168$, or $x = 24$.

23. **Answer: B**

Adding 5 to Larry's money would make the amount of money he has equal to $3x$. Thus, not adding 5 can be represented by $3x - 5$.

24. **Answer: D**

$$15\% = 0.15 \qquad 20\% = 0.2$$
$$30 * 0.15 = 4.5 \qquad 4.5 * 0.2 = 0.9$$

25. **Answer: C**

The formula for the surface area of a sphere is $4\pi r^2$. We know what the surface area is for the sphere, so our equation will look like $4\pi r^2 = 200.96$. We will also replace π with 3.14, so our equation will now look like $4 * 3.14 * r^2 = 200.96$, or $12.56 * r^2 = 200.96$. We now have to isolate r^2, so we divide 12.56 on each side, giving us $r^2 = 16$. Because 4^2 is equal to 16, 4 is the radius of the sphere.

26. **Answer: B**

First, we can isolate x. We are solving for the absolute value so we need to break it into two inequalities.

$-(x - 3) < 2$

Distribute the -1: $-x + 3 < 2$

Subtract 3 on both sides: $-x < -1$

Divide -1 on both sides: $x > 1$

$-(x - 3) > -2$

Distribute the -1: $-x + 3 > -2$

Subtract 3 on both sides: $-x > -5$

Divide -1 on both sides: $x < 5$

In other terms, $1 < x < 5$. The answer cannot be A or D because they have closed circles, which means greater/less than or equal to. $1 < x < 5$ includes the numbers in between 1 and 5, so it must be choice B.

27. **Answer: C**

To find the test score, we need to find the sum of the other tests. To have an average of 86, the sum of the 4 tests needs to be 344. When we subtract the scores of the other tests, 76, 94, and 88, we get 86 which is the final score that Matt needs to get on his final test to have an average of 86 on his tests.

28. **Answer: D**

We can find the value of y by isolating x in equation $x + 2y = 22$, giving us x=22-2y. We now can substitute x in equation $8x + 4y = 92$, giving us $8(22 - 2y) + 4y = 92$. Now we distribute, $176 - 16y + 4y = 92$. We simplify and we get $176 - 12y = 92$. We subtract 176 on each side and we get $-12y = -84$. We divide -12 on each side and we get 7.

29. **Answer: C**

First, we can write out how much Gordon spent in terms of x and y.

One of the multiples of the product is "2 less than three times the amount Dillian spent". We can write this out as $3x - 2$. The other multiple of the product is "5 more than half the amount Matty spent". We can write this out as $\frac{1}{2}y + 5$. Now, we can find the product of the two multiples.

Find the product: $(3x - 2)(\frac{1}{2}y + 5)$

Use FOIL: $\frac{3}{2}xy + 15x - y - 10$ (FOIL because we are multiplying two binomials)

30. **Answer: B**

$0.75 = \frac{3}{4}$ and $0.375 = \frac{3}{8}$, the sum of ¾ and ⅜ is equivalent to $\frac{9}{8}$.

31. **Answer: A**

Since Tim is already 5 years older than Chris and after another 5 years, that will be another plus 5 making A the correct answer.

32. **Answer: C**

We can isolate x.

Divide z on both sides: $32 - 8x = \frac{4y}{z}$

Subtract 32 on both sides: $-8x = \frac{4y}{z} - 32$

Divide -8 on both sides: $x = \frac{4y}{z} \div -\frac{8}{1} - 32 \div -8$ OR

$x = -\frac{4y}{8z} + 4$ OR $x = 4 - \frac{y}{2z}$

33. **Answer: B**

We must first find the prime factorization of each number.

> 12: 2^2 * 3
>
> 15: 3 * 5
>
> 21: 3 * 7

For each unique factor, we find where it appears the most and write it that many times. This would be 2^2 * 3 * 5 * 7. Multiplying this gives us the least common multiple of 420.

34. **Answer: C**

Convert $\frac{35}{6}$ to a mixed number which should be $5\frac{5}{6}$, which is between 5 and 6.

35. **Answer: D**

The total amount has to be a number that is a multiple of 8. Choices A,B, and C are not divisible by 8.

36. **Answer: C**

First, we can simplify the left side of the equation. Using the distributive property of multiplication, $3(9 + 4)$ becomes $3 * 9 + 3 * 4$, or 39.

Alternatively, we can solve the expression in the parentheses first, which becomes $3(13)$ which also equals to 39.

Next, we must isolate the variable, n, by subtracting 3 from both sides of the equation.

After doing this, we have $36 = n^2$. Taking the square root of both sides, we are left with the final answer of $6 = n$, or $n = 6$.

37. **Answer: C**

First, we need to find the total amount of students in all of Mrs. Smith's classes. We know that there are 30 students per class, and she has 4 classes total. We can multiply 30 and 4, giving us a total of 120 students. Now that we have the amount of students, we can multiply by 70%, or 0.7, which gives us a final answer of 84 students passing the class.

38. **Answer: C**

First, we need to find the total amount of inches each grew after 2 months. We know the rate of the elm tree is 5 inches per week. We can multiply 5 by 8, because 8 is the number of weeks in two months, giving us 40. This means the elm tree grew 40 inches in two months.

The oak tree grows at a rate of 0.75 inches per day. Because there are 7 days in a week, we can multiply 0.75 and 7 to find how much the oak tree grows in a week, giving us 5.25 inches. We can then multiply this number by 8, because 8 is the number of weeks in two months, giving us 42. This means the oak tree grew 42 inches in two months.

Finally, we subtract 42 and 40, giving us 2 inches. This is the difference in height after 2 months.

39. **Answer:** B

We can set the equation as 2x + 20 = 180 and solve for x. Subtract 20 from both sides of our equation and our equation would be 2x = 160. Then divide by 2 on both sides of the equation and x equals 80. Since 80 is the interior angle, the exterior angle would be 100 since 180 - 80 = 100.

40. **Answer: B**

We first convert the amount of time it takes Vanessa and Kelly to finish their test into seconds. There are 3600 seconds in an hour. 1.75 * 3600 = 6300 minutes and 3 * 3600 = 10800 minutes. We can now divide how long it takes for them to finish a test by how many questions there are on the test in order to find the amount of time it takes for them to complete one question. $\frac{6300}{40} = \frac{315}{2}$, or 157.5 seconds. $\frac{10800}{40} = 270$ seconds.

Then, we can subtract the two lengths from each other, 270 seconds - 157.5 seconds, giving us 112.5 seconds.

41. **Answer: C**

Explanation: We first simplify the left side of the equation by using the distributive property. This gives us $4y - 28 + 8 - 48y = 24$. We then combine the like terms, giving us $-44y - 20 = 24$. Adding 20 to both sides of the equation gives us $-44y = 44$. Dividing both sides by -44 gives us our final answer of $y = -1$.

42. **Answer: D**

First, we can find how many coins are equal to one bill. 4 times 0.25 equals one, so If $1\ coin = 0.25\ bill$, then we have to multiply 4 on both sides:$1 * 4\ coin = 0.25 * 4\ bill$, or 4 coins = 1 bill.

With this new rate, we can find how much 15 bills are by multiplying 15 to both sides of the rate, $4 * 15\ coins = 0.25 * 15\ bill$, or 60 coins = 15 bills.

43. **Answer: A**

1) $\frac{5}{3} + \frac{10}{3} * \frac{22}{15}$ *Rewrite the mixed number as an improper fraction*

2) $\frac{5}{3} + \frac{10*22}{3*15}$

$\frac{5}{3} + \frac{220}{45}$ *PEMDAS: Multiply numerators and denominators*

3) $\frac{5*15}{3*15} + \frac{220}{45}$

$\frac{75}{45} + \frac{220}{45}$ *Rewrite with least common denominator (LCM = 45)*

4) $\frac{295}{45}$ *Add fractions*

5) $\frac{295 \div 5}{45 \div 5}$ *Simplify using greatest common factor (GCF = 5)*

$\frac{59}{9}$ *Final answer.*

44. **Answer: D**

1) $10n + 20 = 8n$ *Distribute*

2) $20 = -2n$ *Isolate variable*

$n = -10$ *Final answer*

45. **Answer: A**

Since we are looking for the value of x in terms of y and z, we can isolate x:

Add y on each side: $6x = 3z + y$

Divide 6 on each side: $x = \frac{3z + y}{6}$

Simplify: $x = \frac{3z}{6} + \frac{y}{6}$

Simplify: $x = \frac{z}{2} + \frac{y}{6}$

46. **Answer: C**

If the area of one of the cube faces is 5, then the sides must be equal to $\sqrt{5}$. The formula of the volume of a cube is $side\ length^3$, or $\sqrt{5}^3$, or $5\sqrt{5}$.

47. **Answer: D**

We set up a proportion: $\frac{8}{3} = \frac{56}{x}$. We can simplify 8 and 56, giving us $\frac{1}{3} = \frac{7}{x}$, we cross multiply to get x=21, 21 cups.

48. **Answer: D**

Choices A and C are not prime numbers since both of them can be divisible by 3. D is the correct answer because 23 is less than 43.

49. **Answer: D**

The mode of a set is the number that shows up the most frequently. Since 77 shows up 3 times, which is 2 more times more than all the other numbers, the mode of the set is 77.

50. **Answer: A**

The area of a parallelogram is base * height. Because we know the base length, which is 20cm, we can divide that by the area, giving us 11, meaning 11 is the measure of the height. Because AB+BC must equal to the height, or 11, we can rewrite that as

$$2(x - 3) + (x + 2) = 11$$
$$2x - 6 + (x + 2) = 11$$
$$3x - 4 = 11$$
$$3x = 15$$
$$x = 5$$

51. **Answer: D**

By using PEMDAS, we start off with multiplication and $\frac{1}{10} \times \frac{1}{6} = \frac{1}{60}$, and we convert $4\frac{2}{3}$ into $\frac{280}{60}$ and finally, move onto adding $\frac{280}{60}$ and $\frac{1}{60}$ which is $\frac{281}{60}$.

52. **Answer: D**

    1) $2y = -19 - 7x$ *Isolate y in first expression*

    2) $2y = 21 + x$ *Isolate y in second expression*

    3) $21 + x = -19 - 7x$ *Both expressions equal 2y*

    4) $x = -40 - 7x$

    $8x = -40$

    $x = -5$ *Solve for x*

    5) $2y = 21 + (-5)$ *Plug in x*

    6) $2y = 16$

    $y = 8$ *Solve for y*

    $(-5, 8)$ *Final answer*

53. **Answer: C**

Probability is calculated part over the total. After adding three markers in, the total is now 23. The number of blue markers Jake has is still 9. $\frac{9}{23}$

54. **Answer: D**

To solve for x, we isolate x on the left-hand side of the equation. First, we multiply 3 to both sides of the equation. Next, subtract 9 from both sides of the equation. Our equation is now 5x= 48. Finally, divide both sides of the equation by 5. x = 9.6.

55. **Answer: B**

The formula for the surface area of a sphere is $4\pi r^2$. We know what the surface area is for the sphere, so our equation will look like $4\pi r^2 = 200.96$. We will also replace π with 3.14, so our equation will now look like $4 * 3.14 * r^2 = 314$, or $12.56 * r^2 = 314$. We now have to isolate r^2, so we divide 12.56 on each side, giving us $r^2 = 25$. Because 5^2 is equal to 25, 5 is the radius of the sphere. We then multiply it by 2 to get the diameter.

Practice Test #3 Answers:

1. **Answer: 10**

   To find the number of multiples of 6 between 20 and 80, we can find the closest number to 20 that's a multiple of 6 and greater than 20, and the closest number to 80 that's a multiple of 6 and less than 80. The numbers would be 24 and 78, which are 6*4 and 6*13. We can find the number of multiples of 6 between 20 and 80 by subtracting 13 and 4, and adding one back to include the smallest number. This results in an answer of 10.

   Alternatively, you can list out the multiples of 6 between 20 and 80, which are 24, 30, 36, 42, 48, 54, 60, 66, 72, 78. When you count them, you end up with a total of 10 multiples.

2. **Answer: 25**

   First, we have to set up a system of equations. Assume t is the number of tables and c is the number of chairs.

   $$t + 6c = 300$$
   $$2t + 3c = 375$$

   We need to multiply/divide one of the equations, so the two equations share the same variable and coefficient.

   Multiply $t + 6c = 300$ by 2: $2t + 12c = 600$

   Now, we can cancel 2t out in both equations:

   $$2t + 12c = 600$$
   $$- \quad (2t + 3c = 375)$$
   $$\text{------------------------}$$
   $$9c = 225 \text{ OR } c=25$$

   $25 is the cost of one chair.

3. **Answer: 105**

   First, we can find the value of x by using the equation 4x+2x+90=180 (Angle DAB is equal to 90). x will equal 15. 4*15 is equal to 60.

   Now, we can find what 5x is equal to, 5*15=75. Because angle ABC is also equal to 90, we can find what angle COB is equal to 75+90+y=180, or y=15.

   Now we can find what the value of angle b is 60+15+b=180 or b=105.

4. **Answer: 96**

   There are 1,440 minutes in one day. Because the song plays every 15 minutes, we can divide 1,440 by 15 to find how much the song plays each day, which will be 96 times.

5. **Answer: 16**

   Set up inequality as such 20x > 310. X represents the number of hours he has to work. Divide both sides by 20 and the equation will be x > 15.5. As a result, x rounds up to 16.

6. **Answer: D**

   First, we need to find how many feet Sam walks in a minute. We can multiply 4.4 by 60 (the number of seconds in a minute) and we get 264 feet. We then divide 3,168 by 264 to find how many minutes it takes for Sam to walk home. We get 12 minutes.

7. **Answer: A**

   There are 300 more girls than boys, so B + 300 = G. The ratio between boys to girls is 3:4, so G = $\frac{4}{3}$B. B+300 = $\frac{4}{3}$ B. Isolating the variable, B = 900. Plug B into the first equation: 900+300 = G = 1200. Add G and B, 1200 + 900 = 2100

8. **Answer: D**

   We then write out each unique prime factor, based on the number where it appears the most. Thus, we would write 2^4 * 3^2. Multiplying this gives us the least common multiple of the three numbers, which is 144.

9. **Answer: D**

   $3^x = 27^3 = (3^3)^2$ so $3^x = 3^6$ therefore $x = 6$.

10. **Answer: C**

   First, move the variable to the left side of the equation by subtracting 3x from both sides of the equation and then the inequality will be 2x + 1 < 17. Next, subtract 1 from both sides of the equation so the inequality will be 2x < 16. Finally, divide both sides of the inequality by 2 making the inequality: x < 8. The greatest possible value that is less than 8 is 7.

11. **Answer: A**

   We need to find the unit price, meaning we need to find the price of one battery. We can find the unit price by dividing the price of the packs by the number of batteries it holds.

   $5.40 \div 3 = 1.80$ and $18 \div 15 = 1.20$.

   These are the unit prices for the packs. We can now subtract them from each other. 1.80-1.20 = $0.60

12. **Answer: B**

   First, we can find the radius of the circle. Since the formula of the circumference is $2\pi r$, after replacing the given numbers we get, $2\pi r = 8\pi$. Divide 2π on each side and we get r=4. Because the circle is inscribed inside of the square, the diameter is equal to one of the sides of the square. 2*4=8. 8 is the length of one side. We can then multiply 8 by 4 because we need to find the total length of all the sides (the perimeter), and we will get 32 inches.

13. **Answer: D**

First, we find the total number of gumballs in the jar by adding all of them together, which will give us 38 gumballs. Then we find the probability of the gumball being red by creating a fraction with the number of red gumballs as the numerator and the total number of gumballs as the denominator, giving us $\frac{12}{38}$.

After simplifying the fraction by 2, we get our answer $\frac{6}{19}$.

14. **Answer: D**

The numbers that are from 30 to 70 that are multiples of 4 are 32,36,40,44,48,52,56,60,64,68. These are 10 different numbers.

15. **Answer: A**

Distribute: $28 + 32x - 22 + 3x$

Combine like terms: $6 + 35x$

16. **Answer: D**

In an isosceles triangle, two sides will always have the same length, and two angles will have the same measure. If one of the angles equals 30 degrees, we can set up the equation as 2x + 30 = 180. Subtract 30 from both sides of the equation then divide by 2 to solve for x. x = 75.

17. **Answer: C**

To isolate x, we subtract 2y on both sides of the equation, where we end up getting 5x=15-2y. We then divide 5 into both sides which now gives us, $x = \frac{15-2y}{5}$.

We simplify by dividing 15 and -2y by 5 and we finally get our answer, $x = 3 - \frac{2}{5}y$.

18. **Answer: C**

    When 99 is divided by 7, there will be a remainder. When 104 is divided by 7, there will also be a remainder. When 119 is divided by 7, there won't be a remainder.

19. **Answer: D**

    The formula of the volume of a rectangular prism is *width * length * height*. Because the length of rectangular prism is half as much as the height, it will be $\frac{1}{2}$ * 4, or 2. Because the width is three times as large as the length, it will be *2 * 3* or 6. Now that we have our width, length and height, we can replace them in our formula: 2 * 4 * 6 or 48 cubic centimeters.

20. **Answer: A**

    45% of 700 can be found by multiplying 700 by .45. 700 × .45 is equal to 315. 20% of 315 can be found by multiplying 315 by .2. This will result in an answer of 63.

21. **Answer: C**

    We can set up an equation for proportion, which would be $\frac{.6}{10} = \frac{x}{80}$ and solve for x. Next, we cross multiply 80 and .6 along with 10 and x to get the equation 48 = 10x and then solve for x, which is 4.8.

22. **Answer: C**

    We can first simplify the right side of the equation, by taking the negative cube root of 27. This leaves us with $5n^3 - 323 = -3$. We can then add 323 to both sides of the equation to get $5n^3 = 320$. Dividing both sides by 5 leaves us with $n^3 = 64$. To isolate the variable, we can take the cube root of both sides, leaving us with $n = 4$.

23. **Answer: A**

We can first factor the number 48. This gives us $1, 2, 3, 4, 6, 8, 12, 16, 24, 48$. As there are no factors greater than 24, but less than 48, our answer is 0 factors.

24. **Answer: C**

First, we can find out what a is equal to.

Subtract 9 on both sides: $a = 14$

Then, we can find what b is equal to.

Subtract 9 on both sides: $\frac{14}{b} = 7$

Divide 14 on both sides: $\frac{1}{b} = \frac{7}{14}$

Find the reciprocal of both fractions: $b = \frac{14}{7}$

Simplify: $b = 2$

Now, we can find what $4a + 3b$ is now that we know the value of a and b.

Substitute: $4(14) + 3(2)$

Multiply: $56 + 6 = 62$

25. **Answer: B**

The diameter of the globe (which is a sphere), is 6 inches tall, so the radius of the sphere is 3 inches. Using the volume formula for a sphere, $\frac{4}{3}\pi r^3$, or $\frac{4}{3} * 3.14 * r^3$ once we have replaced pi, we can now find the volume: $\frac{4}{3} * 3.14 * 3^3$ or 113.04

26. **Answer: D**

We want to find how many hours it takes Ted to mow the 4,856.25 yard lawn, or $\frac{4,856.25\ yards}{x\ hour}$. From the given information, we know that Ted's rate is $\frac{2,775\ yards}{3\ hours}$. Because these two rates must be equal to each other, we can make an equation: $\frac{4,856.25\ yards}{x\ hour} = \frac{2,775\ yards}{3\ hours}$. We can then cross multiply and find x. $14,568.75 = 2,775x$ or $5.25 = x$. This means it takes 5.25 hours for Ted to mow the 4,856.25 yard lawn.

Because we have to express the answer in hours and minutes, we have to find what 0.25 is in minutes. There are 60 minutes in an hour. We can multiply 60 and 0.25, giving us 15. So, our answer is 5 hours and 15 minutes.

27. **Answer: C**

1) $5x - 5x + 4y - 2y = -7 + 1$

$0 + 2y = -6$ *Add equations*

2) $2y = -6$

$y = -3$ *Solve for y*

3) $-5x - 2(-3) = 1$ *Plug in variable*

4) $-5x + 6 = 1$

$-5x = -5$ *Solve for x*

$x = 1$ *Final answer*

28. **Answer: A**

You can find 30% of 260 by multiplying .3 and 260 which equals 78. Then multiply 78 by 4.

29. **Answer: A**

Explanation: We can first subtract 4 from both sides to get $x^2 = 49$. After taking the square root of both sides of the equation we get $x = 7$.

30. **Answer: B**

The numbers you can roll in a dice are 1,2,3,4,5, and 6. The range of numbers inclusive are 1 and 6. This means that there needs to be an less than or equal to sign in the inequality.

31. **Answer: C**

We are looking for a in terms of b. We first have to isolate a:

Subtract 8b on each side: $-7a = 42 - 8b$

Divide -7 on each side: $a = \frac{42-8b}{-7}$

Simplify: $a = -6 + \frac{8b}{7}$

32. **Answer: C**

There are 13 hearts and 13 diamonds in a deck of 52 cards. The probability of choosing a heart is $\frac{1}{4}$ and choosing a diamond is $\frac{1}{4}$ and you multiply them to find the chance when both are drawn.

33. **Answer: B**

Since angles AOC and BOD are vertically opposite angles, they are equal to each other. As a result, $64 = 7x + 1$ and we just need to solve for x. Subtract one from both sides of the equation and then divide both sides by 7, so x equals 9.

34. **Answer: A**

1) $25\% = \frac{1}{4}$

$\frac{17}{14} * \frac{22}{3} * \frac{1}{4}$ 　　　　　　　　　*Simplify the expression*

2) $\frac{17*22*1}{14*3*4}$

$\frac{374}{168}$ 　　　　　　　　　*Multiply fractions*

3) $\frac{374\div2}{168\div2}$ 　　　　　　*Simplify using greatest common factor (GCF = 2)*

4) $\frac{187}{84}$ 　　　　　　　　　*Final answer.*

35. **Answer: C**

An equation that can be set up is x + (x + 2) = 168 which simplifies to 2x + 2 = 168. We subtract 2 from both sides of the equation and our equation is now 2x = 166. Next, divide both sides of the equation by 2 to get x = 83. The even number that follows 83 is 85.

36. **Answer: C**

Given the ratio of 3:4, the ratio of girls to the total number of the team is 4:7. We can set up a proportion to find the actual number of girls: $\frac{4}{7} = \frac{x}{21}$. We can now cross multiply and find x. $7x = 84$, or x=12. There are 12 girls on the team.

37. **Answer: A**

   First, we can distribute the -1.

   Distribute: $18a - 12 + 3a - 9 = 3b$

   Divide each side by 3: $6a - 4 + a - 3 = b$

   Combine like terms: $7a - 7 = b$

   Now, we can isolate a.

   Add -7 on each side: $7a = b + 7$

   Divide 7 on each side: $a = \frac{b+7}{7}$

   Simplify: $a = \frac{b}{7} + \frac{7}{7}$ or $a = \frac{b}{7} + 1$

38. **Answer: D**

   The possible one digits for numbers that have 7 as the base include 1,7,9 and 3 which is only four numbers. Divide the exponent by 4 and you should be three numbers after the first one. Three numbers after the possible numbers as our one digit is 3.

39. **Answer: C**

   The surface area of a cube can be found using the expression $6a^2$, which represents the length of a side. Surface Area = $6(8)^2$. Surface Area = 384.

40. **Answer: B**

   We first cross-multiply to get $32x = 24$. We can then divide 32 from both sides. We get $x = \frac{24}{32}$, which simplifies to our final answer of $\frac{3}{4}$.

41. **Answer: B**

   After plugging 5 into the expression, the expression will equal 5. 75 - 15 = 60.

42. **Answer: C**

Our proportion looks like the following: 56:48:64:70. We add up all of the numbers, and we get 238. Our proportion of freshman to total student population is 70:238. Since both of the numbers are divisible by 14, it can be simplified to 5:17, which is C.

43. **Answer: B**

By applying the rules of PEMDAS, we need to solve everything inside the parentheses making the equation $2(\frac{1}{8})^2 x = \frac{1}{2}$. $2(\frac{1}{8})^2$ simplifies to $\frac{1}{32}$. Finally we need to solve for $\frac{1}{32}x$. $= \frac{1}{2}$. Multiply both sides by 32 to get x = 16.

44. **Answer: B**

First, we can simplify the right side of the equation, by first either solving the expression in the parentheses or by using the distributive property. Regardless of method, we are left with $2^x - 5 = 11$. We can then add 5 to both sides of the equation, to get $2^x = 16$. Because the method of solving exponents using logarithms is not yet known, we can simply use a table of powers of 2. $2^1 = 2, 2^2 = 4, 2^3 = 8, 2^4 = 16$. Thus, our answer is $x = 4$.

45. **Answer: D**

We can set up an equation of 3x + 8x = 88 and solve for x. Once we solve for x, x is equal to 8. Since we are looking for the number of girls in the class, we just multiply 8 by 8.

46. **Answer: C**

First, we find the prime factorization of 498. This is equal to 2 * 3 * 83. The greatest prime factor of 498 is thus 83.

47. **Answer: D**

We can start with our first equation: "pay a flat fee of $30 and pay $3 every mile you bike OR you can just pay $5 for each mile biked".

$30 will be constant, because you will always pay $30, no matter how much you bike. $3 will be the coefficient because for every mile biked, you pay $3. The equation will look like: $30 + 3x = y$

Then, we can find our second equation: "you can just pay $5 for each mile biked". $5 will be the coefficient because for every mile biked, you pay $5. The equation will look like: $5x = y$

Our system will look like:

$$30 + 3x = y$$
$$5x = y$$

But because there is no exact equivalent to our system in the answers, we have to find what x is equal to in terms of y.

Isolate 3x: $3x = y - 30$

Divide 3 on each side: $x = \frac{y-30}{3}$

The answer is D.

48. **Answer: C**

First, we can cross-multiply to get $-2x = 2(x - 2x)$. We can then distribute to get $-2x = 2x - 4x$. Simplifying this, we get that $-2x = -2x$. This means that for any value of x, our equation will be true. Thus, the value of x can be any real number.

49. **Answer: B**

Assuming x is equal to the side length of the cube, the formula of a square is x^3. If $x^3 = 216$, then x must equal to 6 inches. Because we are looking for one of the faces (which are all the same on the cube), we can find the area by multiplying one side length by another, or 6*6, or 36 square inches.

50. **Answer: D**

Explanation: We can first simplify the right side of the equation. $2^2 - 1$ becomes $4 - 1$, which is equal to 3. After this, we have $\sqrt{18y} = 3$. We can square both sides to isolate the variable, leaving us with $18y = 9$. We can then divide both sides of the equation by 18 to get $y = \frac{9}{18}$, which simplifies into $y = \frac{1}{2}$.

51. **Answer: D**

Explanation:

1) $(25\,mph * 2\,hours) + (35\,mph * x\,hours) = 120\,miles$ *Set up equation*

2) $(25 * 2) + (35x) = 120$

$50 + 35x = 120$

$35x = 70$ *Solve for x*

$x = 2$ hours   *Final answer*

52. **Answer: B**

After the raise, Timothy earns $23 an hour. 20 * 1.15 = 23. After 5 hours, he would earn $115. If he works 5 hours with his old salary, he earns only $100. 115 - 100 = 15.

53. **Answer: C**

1/5 is equal to 0.2. Since 0.23 is greater than 0.2, C is the correct answer.

54. **Answer: C**

To isolate y, add 8x to both sides of the equation. Our equation should now be - 9y=17+8x. Divide by -9 to solve for y, and our equation should be $y = -\frac{17+8x}{9}$.

55. **Answer: B**

There are 12 inches in a foot, so 6^x must be equal to 36. 6^4 is equal to 36, so 4 is equal to x.

Practice Test #4 Answers:

1. **Answer: 6**

   We can set up an equation: x(x+1)(x+2) = 210. After simplifying: $x^3 + 3x^2 + 2x = 210$. Then, we solve for x by subtracting 210 from both sides to get the equation: $x^3 + 3x^2 + 2x - 210 = 0$. We can factor the equation into $(x - 5)(x^2 + 8x + 42)$ and find the solution x=5. The second answer would then equal 6.

2. **Answer: 236**

   The volume of a cylinder is represented by $v = \pi r^2 h$. We know the height and radius, which allows us to find the volume. The volume is 785.4. 30% of 785.4 is 235.62, which rounds up to 236.

3. **Answer: 225**

   Since we know 135 is the complementary angle to one of the angles in the parallelogram, we can subtract 135 from 180, giving us 45 degrees. In a parallelogram, the opposite angles are equal, so 45 must equal to y. Because 135 and angle x are interior alternate angles, they must be equal.
   Now that we know what x and y are equal to, we can substitute: 2(135)-45, which is equal to 225 degrees.

4. **Answer: 5**

   Our first step is to simplify both sides of the equation using the distributive property of multiplication. This leaves us with $3x + 12 = 9x - 18$. We can then subtract $3x$ from both sides of the equation, leaving us with $12 = 6x - 18$. To isolate the variable, we can add 18 to both sides of the equation, which gives us $6x = 30$. We can then divide both sides by 6 which leaves us with our final answer of $x = 5$.

5. **Answer: 1890**

   To solve 40% of 4200, we can multiply 4200 by 0.4. $4200 \times .4$ is equal to 1680. 25% of 1680 is equal to multiplying 1680 by 0.25. $1680 \times .25$ is equal to 420.

6. **Answer: A**

   First, we can simplify the left side of the equation by using the distributive property of multiplication. This gives us $8x + 36 + 3x = 38$. We can combine the like terms on the left side to get $11x + 36 = -8$. Then, we subtract 36 from both sides of the equation to get $11x = 44$. Dividing both sides by 11 yields the final answer of $x = -4$.

7. **Answer: A**

   Define variables:

   d=Distance traveled by the passenger train before being caught up with

   x=Time traveled by the passenger train

   Thus,

   $x - 3$ =Time traveled by the cattle train

   $$d = Speed * Time$$

   Passenger train: $d = 56km/h * x$

   Cattle train: $d = 80km/h * (x - 3)$

   $80 * (x - 3) = 56x$ *Both values equal to d*

   1) $80x - 240 = 56x$

   $-240 = -24x$ *Solve for x*

   $x = 10\ hours$ *Final answer*

8. **Answer: D**

   The equation for the surface area of a cube is $6a^2$. Plug $4x^3$ as a $.6 \times 16 = 96$ and $(x^3)^3 = x^6$.

9. **Answer: C**

   We must first find the prime factorization of each number.

   > 3: 3
   > 8: 2^3
   > 14: 2 * 7

   For each unique factor, we find where it appears the most and write it that many times.

   This would be 2^3 * 3 * 7. Multiplying this gives us the least common multiple of 168.

10. **Answer: D**

    The tree is 3 meters tall, which we can convert to 300 centimeters. We add 64 centimeters and get 364 meters. We can set up an equation: 364=300x. We solve for x and get 1.2133, which we subtract 1 from and get 0.2133. Then, we can convert 0.2133 to 21.33%.

11. **Answer: C**

    David's score is 100. To find the median, we find the mean of the 2 numbers in the middle of the set. We get a median of 90 and subtract it from David's score to get an answer of 10.

12. **Answer: B**

Explanation:

1) $\frac{x-7}{6} = \frac{-11}{4}$ *Distribute negative*

2) $-11(6) = 4(x - 7)$ *Cross-multiply*

3) $-66 = 4x - 28$

$4x = -38$ *Solve for x*

$x = -\frac{38}{4}$

$x = -\frac{19}{2}$

$x = -9\frac{1}{2}$

$x = -9.5$ *Final answer*

13. **Answer: B**

If n were 3, any odd number multiplied by an even number outputs an even number. As a result, A, C, and D are wrong.

14. **Answer: B**

Finding 250% of a number is the same as multiplying the given number by 2.5 . $2.5 * 150 = 375$.

15. **Answer: D**

   We need to find the value of a before we can find what half of a is equal to. We isolate a.

   Subtract $\frac{3}{4}b$ on both sides: $\frac{1}{8}a = 34 - \frac{3}{4}b$

   Multiply 8 on both sides: $a = 272 - 6b$

   Now that we know what a is equal to, we can multiply both sides by $\frac{1}{2}$.

   Multiply by $\frac{1}{2}$: $\qquad \frac{1}{2}a = \frac{1}{2}(272 - 6b)$

   Simplify: $\frac{1}{2}a = 136 - 3b$

16. **Answer: D**

   We can first add 7 to both sides, giving us $5n = n + 6$. Subtracting n from both sides gives us $4n = 6$. We can then divide both sides of the equation by 4 to get $n = \frac{6}{4}$, which simplifies to $n = \frac{3}{2}$.

17. **Answer: C**

   1) Reciprocal of $\frac{1}{6} = 6$

   Reciprocal of $4 = \frac{1}{4}$ *Find reciprocals.*

   2) $6 + \frac{1}{4}$

   $6\frac{1}{4}$

   $\frac{25}{4}$ *Add*

   3) Reciprocal of $\frac{25}{4} = \frac{4}{25}$ *Find reciprocal - Final answer*

18. **Answer: C**

Because we know the perimeter is 154 inches, the perimeter in ratio form would be 14 (the perimeter is 2*length + 2*width, or 5*2+2*2 with the ratio numbers). We can set up a proportion: $\frac{5}{14} = \frac{x}{154}$. x=55. 55 will be the length of the rectangle. We can subtract 55*2, or 110, from the perimeter, giving us 44. 44, which is two times the width. We can divide 44.44 by 2 and get 22. This is the width of the rectangle.

19. **Answer: C**

1) $2y = -10$

$y = -5$ *Solve for y*

2) $5x + 4(-5) = 20$ *Plug in y*

3) $5x - 20 = 20$

$5x = 40$

$x = 8$ *Solve for x*

$(8, -5)$ *Final answer*

20. **Answer: A**

This word problem can be represented by the equation $0.06 = \frac{x}{50}$. We can then multiply both sides by 50 to get our final answer of $x = 3$.

21. **Answer: B**

15% of a certain amount is the same as multiplying by .85. $120 \times .85$ is equal to 102. Since there is tax, there would be an increase. You can find the price after tax by finding the product of 1.09 and 102.

22. **Answer: B**

First, we set the value of b in the ratio 21:27 equal to the value of b in the ratio 3:7. We divide 21 by 3 because it gives us 7. Because we divided one side of the ratio, we must divide the other side by 3 to keep the ratio equal. Our new ratio is 7:9. We now add the ratio numbers to find the total, 3+7+9=19. We can set up a proportion to find the actual value of b and solve for x: $\frac{x}{95} = \frac{7}{19}$, $19x = 665$, or x=35. The value of b is 35.

23. **Answer: B**

The values of x include 1 and -1, which means the greater than and equal to sign, as well as the less than and equal to sign, must be used. Since the range is both from -1 to -infinity and 1 to infinity, the answer is B.

24. **Answer: A**

First, we can multiply both sides of the equation by $2x + 7$. This gives us $14 = 4(2x + 7)$. Then, we can use the distributive property of multiplication to simplify the right side of the equation. This gives us $14 = 8x + 28$. After this, we isolate the variable by subtracting 28 from both sides. This gives us $-14 = 8x$. We then divide both sides of the equation by 8, leaving us with $x = \frac{-14}{8}$. Simplifying this fraction gives us our final answer of $x = \frac{-7}{4}$.

25. **Answer: B**

1) $(17mph * 10\ hours) + (x\ mph * 10\ hours) = 320\ miles$ *Set equation*

2) $(17 * 10) + (10x) = 320$

$170 + 10x = 320$

$10x = 150$ *Solve for x*

$x = 15$ mph   *Final answer*

26. **Answer: D**

   First, we need to convert the height, width, and length into inches. The height is 24 inches, the width is 36 inches, and the length is 36 inches. The product of 24, 36, and 36 is 31,104.

27. **Answer: A**

   All even numbers are not prime so that eliminates choice B. If a number can be divided by 3 without a remainder, then the number isn't a prime number, which eliminates C and D.

28. **Answer: A**

   We can first simplify the left side of the equation. $4(3) = 4 * 3 = 12$. We thus get $12 = \frac{6}{y} - 3$. We can add 3 to both sides of the equation to get $15 = \frac{6}{y}$. Multiplying by y on both sides results in $15y = 6$. To isolate the variable, we can divide both sides of the equation by 15 to get $y = \frac{6}{15}$. This can be simplified to our final answer of $y = \frac{2}{5}$.

29. **Answer: A**

   There are 16 ounces in a pound. Because 5 ounces is not enough to be a full pound, we can find how much it weighs in terms of pounds by dividing it: $\frac{5}{16}$.

30. **Answer: B**

1) $\left(4(\frac{3*7}{4*7} + \frac{3*4}{7*4})\right)/9$

$\left(4(\frac{21}{28} + \frac{12}{28})\right)/9$

$(4 * \frac{33}{28})/9$ *Add fractions in numerator.*

2) $\frac{4*33}{1*28}/9$

$\frac{132}{28}/9$ *Multiply fractions.*

3) $\frac{132}{28} * \frac{1}{9}$

$\frac{132*1}{28*9}$

$\frac{132}{252}$ *Divide fractions: Multiply by reciprocal.*

4) $\frac{132÷12}{252÷12}$ *Simplify using greatest common factor (GCF = 12)*

$\frac{11}{21}$ *Final answer.*

31. **Answer: A**

The formula for the volume of a right circular cone is $V = \frac{1}{3}r^2h\pi$. We can solve for the radius by dividing the diameter by 2. The height is given. Plug the height and radius into the equation and our volume will be 25.12.

32. **Answer: C**

If the pitcher holds 2.4 liters and 40% spills out, 60% of the water remains in the pitcher. We can multiply 2.4 liters by 60% to find how much water remains in the pitcher, giving us 1.44 liters. 14.4 deciliters is the only answer choice that equals to 1.44 liters.

33. **Answer: A**

   We need to isolate a to find its value in terms of b.

   Subtract 7b: $40 - 7b = -10a$

   Divide -10 from both sides: $-4 + \frac{7}{10}b = a$

34. **Answer: A**

   First, we can figure out the measure of angle B by setting up the equation: 2x + 50 = 180. Subtract 50 from both sides of the equation and then divide by 2. As a result, x = 65. Since angle B is an interior angle, the exterior angle (angle A) is now 115, since 180 − 65 = 115. Plug A and B into the expression 2(115) - 65 = 165.

35. **Answer: A**

   3x + 3 = 168. To solve for x, we need to subtract 3 from both sides of the equation to get 3x = 165. Next, we just need to divide both sides of the equation by 3. As a result, x = 55.

36. **Answer: A**

   1) $4(5k - 1) = 7(5k - 10)$ *Cross-multiply*

   2) $20k - 4 = 35k - 70$

   $-4 = 15k - 70$

   $66 = 15k$ *Solve for k*

   $k = \frac{66}{15}$

   $k = \frac{22}{5}$

   $k = 4\frac{2}{5}$

   $k = 4.4$ *Final answer*

37. **Answer: D**

There are 6 different ways to arrange the algebra textbooks, since 3! = 3 x 2 x 1 = 6. There are 120 different ways to arrange the geometry textbooks, since 5! = 5 x 4 x 3 x 2 x1 = 120. Since they are on two different shelves, they can be rearranged in 720 different ways, because 6 x 120 = 720.

38. **Answer: D**

The given problem can be written as $\frac{25}{100}x = 5500$, since 25% is equal to $\frac{25}{100}$. This can be further simplified to $\frac{1}{4}x = 5500$. We can then divide both sides of the equation by $\frac{1}{4}$, which is the same as multiplying both sides of the equation by 4. We are then left with our final answer of $x = 22,000$.

39. **Answer: B**

First, we can simplify both sides of the equation. For the left side of the equation, we can add $\sqrt{2+7}$ to get $\sqrt{9}$, which can be simplified to 3. For the right side of the equation, we can simplify $2 * 3^2$ into $2 * 9$, which is equal to 18. We are left with $\frac{5y}{3} = \frac{5}{18}$. Then, we can cross multiply to get $90y = 15$. To isolate the variable, we divide both sides of the equation by 90. We are left with $y = \frac{15}{90}$. As the question asks for the answer in simplest form, we must simplify the fraction. This yields the final answer of $y = \frac{1}{6}$.

40. **Answer: B**

We must find the prime factorization of 90. This would be 2 * 3 * 3 * 5, which written in exponential form is 2 * 3^2 *5.

41. **Answer: D**

The area of a circle is $r^2\pi$. Because we know $r^2 = 16$, r must equal to 4. This means that the radius of the circles is 4 inches.

The diameter of the circle is equal to side BD, so 2*4 =8.

The value of two diameters is equal to side AB, so 4*4=16.

Now that we have two sides of the rectangle, we can find the area 8*16 or 128 square inches.

42. **Answer: D**

1) $4(5x + 1) = 8(x - 6)$ *Cross-multiply*

2) $20x + 4 = 8x - 48$

$20x = 8x - 52$

$12x = -52$ *Solve for x*

$x = -\dfrac{52}{12}$

$x = -\dfrac{13}{3}$

$x = -4\dfrac{1}{3}$

$x = -4.33$ *Final answer*

43. **Answer: A**

1) $\frac{91}{49}\left(\frac{3}{5}\right) + \frac{8}{5}$

   Plug in variable

2) $\frac{91*3}{49*5} + \frac{8}{5}$

   $\frac{273}{245} + \frac{8}{5}$

   Multiply numerators and denominators

   $\frac{273}{245} + \frac{8*49}{5*49}$

   $\frac{273}{245} + \frac{392}{245}$

   Add fractions using common denominator (LCM = 245)

4) $\frac{273+392}{245}$

   $\frac{665}{245}$

   Add numerators

5) $\frac{665 \div 35}{245 \div 35}$

   Simplify using greatest common factor (GCF = 35)

   $\frac{19}{7}$

   Final answer.

44. **Answer: D**

We know that this triangle is a right triangle. Since we are given the angle of 30°, we can subtract 90° and 30° from 180°, which leaves us with 60°. Since 60° is an interior angle and a° is an exterior angle, we can subtract 60° from 180° to get 120° degrees.

45. **Answer: C**

The total amount of pens there are in the pencil case is 27. There are 21 other pens that are not green. Therefore, the probability is $\frac{21}{27}$, which can be simplified to $\frac{7}{9}$.

46. **Answer: C**

We first simplify the left side to $\frac{2x}{25-11}$, or $\frac{2x}{14}$. We can then cross multiply to get $2x^2 = 98$. Dividing both sides by 2 gives us $x^2 = 49$. Taking the square root of each side gives us our final answer of $x = 7$.

47. **Answer: B**

First, we can set up a system of equations. Assume that x=the number of pencils and y=the number of erasers:

$$5x + 3y = 2.75$$
$$2x + 6y = 3.50$$

We can multiply $5x + 3y = 2.75$ by 2 so both equations share 6y:

$$(5x + 3y = 2.75)\, 2 = 10x + 6y = 5.5$$

Now, we can cancel the two equations out.

$$10x + 6y = 5.5$$
$$-\ (2x + 6y = 3.50)$$

$$8x = 2 \text{ OR } x=0.25$$

This means each pencil costs $0.25.

48. **Answer: B**

Since the area of a square is equal to s^2, the area has to be a square number. Choices A, C, and D are all squares of a number so B is the correct answer.

49. **Answer: B**

Since there is a 40% increase in price, the new price can be solving by 300 x 1.4 which equals 420. Since Brian gets it 20% off, we can figure out the new price by multiplying 420 and .8, which gets us 336.

50. **Answer: A**

There are 3 feet in a yard, and there are 12 inches in a foot. 6 feet and 3 inches would look like $6\frac{3}{12}$ or 6.25 feet in decimal form. We can divide 6.25 feet by 3 feet, in order to find the measure of how tall the man is in yards. We will get $2.08\underline{3}$ yards, or 2.08 yards once we round the number.

51. **Answer: D**

Convert $\frac{88}{9}$ to a mixed number which should be $9\frac{7}{9}$. $9\frac{7}{9}$ is between 9 and 10.

52. **Answer: C**

We have to isolate y.

Subtract $\frac{7x}{2}$ on both sides: $\frac{3}{y} = 84 - \frac{7x}{2}$

Multiply $\frac{1}{3}$ on both sides: $y = \frac{84 - \frac{7x}{2}}{3}$

Simplify: $y = (84 * \frac{1}{3}) - (\frac{7x}{2} * \frac{1}{3})$ or $y = 28 - \frac{7x}{6}$

53. **Answer: B**

When a, b, and c have a common denominator, we need to convert our numerator too. The common denominator will be 819. A will be equal to around .53 b is around .57 and c is equal to .55 repeating.

54. **Answer: C**

Because $10 is the maximum amount of money we can spend, the combination of the tube of glue and the pieces of felt must be less than or equal to 10.

55. **Answer: D**

We can first distribute the left side of the equation. This gives us $5 - 5m - 2 + 2m = 15$. Combining the like terms gives us $3 - 3m = 15$. We can then subtract 3 from both sides of the equation which gives us $-3m = 12$. Dividing both sides by -3 gives us our final answer of $m = -4$.

Practice Test #5 Answers:

1. **Answer: 6600**

   The simple interest formula is I = Prt, which P represents the initial amount, r represents the rate in decimal form, and t represents the years. P = 5000, r = 1.08 and t = 4. I = 5000(0.08)4 which is equal to 1600. 1600 + 5,000 is equal to 6600.

2. **Answer: 7**

   We first distribute the left side of the equation. This gives us $-3y + 3 + 8y - 24 = 6y + 7 - 5y$. Combining the like terms on both sides gets us $5y - 21 = y + 7$. We then add 21 to both sides of the equation which gives us $5y = y + 28$. Subtracting y from both sides gives us $4y = 28$. We then can divide both sides by 4 to get our final answer of $y = 7$.

3. **Answer: 20**

   The angle of a line is equal to 180. We can set up the equation as 3x + 2x + 2x + 2x = 180. After adding all the like terms, our equation is now 9x = 180. Divide 9 on both sides of the equation, and x equals 20.

4. **Answer: 2**

   Use the inverse of operations. If x is divided by 6, and the quotient is 7, then multiply 6 and 7 and add the remainder that was given. The number will be 46. 46 divided by 4 is equal to 11 and the remainder will be 2.

5. **Answer: 15**

   The midpoint of the x-coordinate is the sum of -2 and 8 divided by 2 which is 3 and the midpoint of the y coordinate is the sum 4 and 20 divided by 2 is 12. The sum of 3 and 12 is 15.

6. **Answer: C**

   We must first find the prime factorization of each number.

   28: 2^2 * 7

   48: 2^4 * 3

   For each unique factor, we find where it appears the most and write it that many times.

   This would be 2^4 * 3 * 7. Multiplying this gives us the least common multiple of 336.

7. **Answer: B**

   First, we can isolate b:

   Subtract $\frac{1}{3}a$ on both sides: $\frac{3}{4}b = 21 - \frac{1}{3}a$

   Multiply the reciprocal of $\frac{3}{4}$ on both sides, so the coefficient of b cancels out: $b = 28 - \frac{4}{9}a$

8. **Answer: A**

   The answer will be A because an even integer multiplied by an even integer will always be an even integer.

9. **Answer: C**

   1) $(x\ mph\ *\ (2+3)\ hours)\ =\ ((x+30)\ mph\ *\ 3\ hours)$ *Set equation*

   2) $(2+3)x = 3(x+30)$

   $5x = 3x + 90$

   $2x = 90$ *Solve for x*

   $x = 45$ mph   *Final answer*

10. **Answer: D**

We are given a value of $y = -5$ that we must plug in to the equation in order to solve for x. This gives us $x + 2(-5) = -2(-5) - (x + 14)$. Simplifying this, we get $x - 10 = 10 - (x + 14)$. Distributing the negative gives us $x - 10 = 10 - x - 14$. Simplifying this gets us $x - 10 = -4 - x$. We then must add 10 and x to both sides, which gives us $2x = 6$. Dividing both sides by 2 gives us our final answer of $x = 3$.

11. **Answer: D**

First we find out what x is equal to by using the left triangle. On the left triangle, we are given two angles 15 and 90 since the right triangle has a right angle. To determine what x is, we can set up the equation of 15 + 5x = 90. Then solve for x by subtracting 15 from both sides of the equation and then dividing by 5 which gives x = 15. Then, set up an equation to solve y which would be 90 + 2(15) + y = 180. Subtract 120 from both sides of the equation to get y. y = 60.

12. **Answer: A**

First, we need to find how many weeks are in 2 years.
Since there are 52 weeks in a year, we multiply it by two, which gives us 104 weeks. Because Terrance is going every 8th day, we divide 104 by 8, giving us 13.

13. **Answer: A**

Since there are 60 pigs, 15% more of 60 is 69, and to figure out the number of cows there are, we can subtract 5 from 60. $\frac{part}{total} = \frac{55}{184}$.

14. **Answer: B**

First, subtract 7 from both sides of the inequality. The inequality is now 4x < 28. Then divide both sides of our inequality by 4. As a result, our inequality is x < 7.

15. **Answer: A**

    Put a 1 under 8.375. Since there are 3 digits after the decimal, we multiply the top and top and bottom by 1,000. $\frac{8375}{1,000}$ *can* be simplified to $\frac{67}{8}$.

16. **Answer: C**

    If the diameter is 18cm, then the radius is equal to 9cm. The formula for the volume of a sphere is V = $\frac{4}{3}\pi r^3$. Once we plug 9 as r into the equation, V will equal 3,054 cm^3.

17. **Answer: D**

    We first divide both sides by 0.25, or ¼, which leaves us with n + 8 = 60. Now, we isolate the variable by subracting 8 on both sides, which leaves us with the answer n = 52.

18. **Answer: B**

    The conversion equation of F to C is $(F - 32) \times \frac{5}{9} = C$. Using this equation, 20 C° is 68 F°. 3 times 4.5 is 13.5. So, with this information 68F°- 13.5F°, giving us 54.5F°.

19. **Answer: A**

    We can square both sides: $\sqrt{9x}^2 = 6^2$, giving us $9x = 36$. We can divide 9 on each side, giving us x=4.

20. **Answer: D**

    The equation that can represent the problem is x + (x+1) + (x+2) + (x+3) + (x+4) = 6x. The equation can be simplified as 5x + 10 = 6x. X is equal to 10. The consecutive integers that follow it is 10,11,12,13,14.

21. **Answer: B**

First, subtract 22 from both sides of the equation making the inequality -5x < 3x - 24. Next, subtract 3x from both sides of the inequality. The inequality is now -8x < 24. Dividing by -8 causes us to flip the sign and now our inequality is x > 3.

22. **Answer: A**

1) $\dfrac{-9}{2k-10} = \dfrac{6}{2k+5}$ *Distribute negative sign*

2) $-9(2k+5) = 6(2k-10)$ *Cross-multiply*

3) $-18k - 45 = 12k - 60$

$-18k = 12k - 15$

$-30k = -15$ *Solve for k*

$k = 0.5$ *Final answer*

23. **Answer: B**

1) $2(\frac{3*9}{4*9} + \frac{7*4}{9*4}) * (\frac{1}{2})^2$ *Solve parentheses first - PEMDAS*

$2(\frac{27}{36} + \frac{28}{36}) * (\frac{1}{2})^2$ *Add using common denominator (LCM = 36)*

$2 * \frac{55}{36} * (\frac{1}{2})^2$ *Add numerators*

2) $2 * \frac{55}{36} * \frac{1}{2} * \frac{1}{2}$ *Solve exponent*

3) $\frac{2*55*1*1}{1*36*2*2}$ *Multiply numerators and exponents*

$\frac{2*55}{36*2*2}$

$\frac{110}{144}$

4) $\frac{110 \div 2}{144 \div 2}$ *Simplify using greatest common factor (GCF =2)*

$\frac{55}{72}$ *Final answer.*

24. **Answer: C**

The formula of the surface area of a sphere is $4\pi r^2$. Because the height is 12 inches, 12 would also be the diameter of the circle. The diameter is $2r$, so the radius of the sphere would be 6. Using the given information, our equation to find the surface area would look like $4\pi 6^2$, or $4 * 3.14 * 6^2$ once we replace π with 3.14. Once we multiply them all together, we get 75.36 square inches.

25. **Answer: C**

We need to isolate x.

Divide (x+y) on both sides: $x^2 = \frac{20}{4+y}$

Find the square root of each side: $x = \sqrt{\frac{20}{4+y}}$

26. **Answer: D**

Bicycles have 2 wheels, unicycles only have one wheel, and a tricycle has 3 wheels. ½ of 32 is 16, and 16 times 2 is 32. Since ¼ of her friends own a unicycle, 8 of them own a unicycle which is just 8 wheels in total. The rest of her friends is 8 friends and all of them have a tricycle resulting in 24 wheels. 32 + 8 + 24 is equal to 64.

27. **Answer: C**

b and a are supplementary angles, so when combined they add up to 180 degrees. Knowing this we can make this equation: $(\frac{1}{2}a - 6) + a = 180$. We add 6 on both sides to get 3/2 a = 186. After we divide both sides by 3/2, or multiply by 2/3, we get a=124. Now that we have a, we can plug a into the equation $(\frac{1}{2}a - 6)$, which gets us b = 56.

28. **Answer: A**

Because the absolute value of $5x + 37$ is equal to 12, that means that the expression $5x + 37$ can be equal to either +12, or -12. Thus, the equation must be solved twice to get two answers. Assuming $5x + 37 = 12$, we can subtract 37 from both sides of the equation to get $5x = -25$. Dividing both sides of the equation by 5 leaves us with $x = -5$. Assuming $5x + 37 = -12$, we subtract 37 from both sides of the equation, leaving us with $5x = -49$. Dividing both sides of the equation by 5 leaves us with $x = \frac{-49}{5}$. Because the question asks only for the integer value of x, our answer is $x = -5$

29. **Answer: B**

    To find the percentage we need to figure out how many houses in total there are. We add 2, 5, 8, and 10, which gives us a sum of 25. To find out how many are more than $600,000, we need to add up the number of houses that are more than $600,000, which is 18. Now that we have a number, we can divide 18 by 25, which gives us 0.72, or 72%.

30. **Answer: A**

    If the ratio of A:B is 1:2 and the ratio of B:C is 3:4, then B must equal to B. We can find the greatest common factor of both 2 and 3, which is 6. In order to make B equal to six, we must multiply 1 and 2 by 2 and multiply 3 and 4 by 3. Our new ratio will be 3:6:8. In order to find how much bigger Amount C is to Amount A, we can divide $\frac{8}{3}$, or $2\frac{2}{3}$.

31. **Answer: C**

    1) $-3 + 9x + 7(3 + 6x) = 18$

    $-3 + 9x + 21 + 42x = 18$ *Distribute*

    2) $18 + 9x + 42x = 18$

    $18 + 51x = 18$ *Combine like terms*

    3) $51x = 0$ *Isolate variable*

    $x = 0$ *Final answer*

32. **Answer: B**

    The reciprocal of $\frac{2}{5}$ is $\frac{5}{2}$ so choices A and C are wrong. Plug (2,2) into B or D to determine which is true. $\frac{5}{2}(2) - 3 = 2$ which is true. $\frac{5}{2}(2) - 2 = 2$ is false so B is correct.

33. **Answer: C**

First, we can distribute -3.

Distribute -3: $4a - 2b - 3a + 6 = -62$

Combine like terms: $a - 2b + 6 = -62$

Add 2b to each side: $a + 6 = -62 + 2b$

Subtract 6 from both sides: $a = -68 + 2b$

34. **Answer: D**

1) $x = 17 - 2y$ *Isolate x*

2) $7(17 - 2y) - 2y = 23$ *Plug in x*

3) $119 - 14y - 2y = 23$

$119 - 16y = 23$

$-16y = -96$

$y = 6$ *Solve for variable*

4) $x = 17 - 2(6)$ *Plug in y*

5) $x = 17 - 12$

$x = 5$ *Solve for variable*

$(5,6)$ *Final answer*

35. **Answer: C**

An equation that can be set up as x + (x + 1) = 133 which simplifies to 2x + 1 = 133, We then just isolate x to get x = 66. The greater number is one higher than 66, which is 67.

36. **Answer: D**

Triangle ABC is a right triangle, meaning the missing side of ABC must be 12 cm. If the sides of triangle ABC are 2.5 bigger than the sides of triangle XYZ, we divide the sides of ABC by 2.5 in order to find the sides of triangle XYZ. We need to find the base and height, so we divide 5 and 12 by 2.5, giving us 2 and 4.8 respectively. We multiply them together and divide by 2, getting 4.8 cm.

37. **Answer: B**

The values that x can be are inclusive 1 and 7 which means the greater than and equal to signs as well as the less than and equal to sign have to be used. Since the range can be both 1 to -infinity and 7 to infinity, we need the "and".

38. **Answer: C**

If each digit can only be used once which means no repetition, then this is a permutation problem. There are 5 different digits so we need 5! which is equal to 5 x 4 x 3 x 2 x 1 = 120.

39. **Answer: A**

We can first distribute the left side of the equation, giving us $-2x - 16 - 7x + 7 = -6x$. Combining the like terms gives us $-9x - 9 = -6x$. We must then add $-9x$ to both sides of the equation, giving us $-9 = 3x$. Dividing both sides by 3 gives us our final answer of $x = -3$.

40. **Answer: D**

Finding 30% of 300 is 90 and 30% of 500 is 150. The sum of 150 and 90 is 240.

41. **Answer: B**

First, we can isolate a.

Distribute: $3a + 9c + 12 = 6b$

Subtract 9c on both sides: $3a + 12 = 6b - 9c$

Subtract 12 on both sides: $3a = 6b - 9c - 12$

Divide each side by 3: $a = 2b - 3c - 4$

42. **Answer: D**

To find both possible values, we need to do the absolute value twice, once negative and once positive. We solve -2x + 3 > 11, and we get x < -4. We do it once again, but instead we have -2x + 3 > -11, and we get x < 7. Now that we have our values, we know that our answer is D.

43. **Answer: A**

First, we find how many feet the person runs per hour. Because the rate $(\frac{3}{1})$ is a minute and there are 60 minutes in an hour, we multiply both the number of feet and the minutes by 60, $\frac{180}{60}$. This means the person can run 180 feet in 60 minutes, or 1 hour. We then have to convert the 60 yards into feet. Since there are 3 feet in a yard, we multiply 3 by 60, giving us 180 feet. 180 feet is also the amount of times it takes for that person to run.

44. **Answer: B**

Because the pentagon is regular, all the angles will have the same measure, 108 degrees. In order to find the measure of x, we can find the angles of triangle AED. If angle E is 108, the other two angles must be equal to each other. 72 (supplementary angle of 108) divided by 2 is 36.

45. **Answer: B**

We are dividing mixed numbers, so we have to convert them into fractions. $3\frac{1}{9}$ is $\frac{28}{9}$ and $1\frac{3}{4}$ is $\frac{7}{4}$. We then divide them: $\frac{28}{9} \div \frac{7}{4}$. We are dividing fractions so we find the reciprocal of $\frac{7}{4}$, which is $\frac{4}{7}$, which makes our expression, $\frac{28}{9} \times \frac{4}{7}$. This gives us $\frac{16}{9}$, or $1\frac{7}{9}$.

46. **Answer: A**

First, we simply $6^{-3} * 6^{-2}$. Because we are multiplying exponents we add -3 and -2, giving us -5. Our fraction now looks like $\frac{6^5}{6^{-5}}$. We now divide, meaning we subtract the exponents, giving us our answer, 6^{10}.

47. **Answer: D**

We must first simplify both sides of the equation. On the left side, we distribute to get $25x + 17x - 102 = x(12)^2$. On the right side, we must raise 12 to the second power, giving us $25x + 17x - 102 = 144x$. We then combine the like terms on the left side, which gives us the equation $42x - 102 = 144x$. Subtracting $42x$ from both sides gives us $-102 = 102x$. Dividing both sides by 102 gives us our final answer of $x = -1$.

48. **Answer: B**

Use the inverse of operations. If a is divided by 9, and the quotient is 6, then multiply 9 and 6 and add the remainder that was given. The number will be 61. 61 divided by 4 is equal to 15 and the remainder will be 1.

15 x 1 = 15.

49. **Answer: B**

First, we should convert our measurements into the same unit of measure. Since there are 1,000 meters in 1 kilometer, we multiply 0.032 by 1,000 in order to convert the unit from kilometers to meters, giving us 32. We also convert 1,600 centimeters into meters. Because there are 100 centimeters in a meter, we divide 1,600 by 100, giving us 16. The formula of finding the volume $length \times width \times height = 1,024$. We can replace the length and width values with our converted value: $32 \times 16 \times height = 1,024$ or $512 \times height = 1,024$. We can find the height by dividing 1,024 by 512, giving us 2 meters. 200 centimeters is the only answer that equals 2 meters.

50. **Answer: D**

To find what x is, divide both sides of the equation by ⅔ and x is equal to 75. The product of 75 and 5 is 375.

51. **Answer: C**

After multiplying both sides by -1 which would reverse the inequality, the expression is now 4(x-2) > -4. Then we divide both sides by 4 making the inequality x - 2 > -1 . Then add 2 to both sides of the inequality making the inequality x > 1.

52. **Answer: D**

1) $5x = 5(7x - 2)$ *Cross-multiply*

2) $5x = 35x - 10$

$-30x = -10$ *Solve for x*

$x = \dfrac{-10}{-30}$

$x = \dfrac{1}{3}$

$x = 0.3$ *Final answer*

53. **Answer: A**

We know that 5x-90, 4x and x+30 all add up to 180 degrees. $(5x - 90) + 4x + (x + 30) = 180$. Now, we can solve for x. x=24.

54. **Answer: D**

Solve using elimination

1) $(-7x + 9x) + (8y - 8y) = (9 - 7)$ *Add equations together*

$2x + 0 = 2$

2) $2x = 2$ *Solve for x*

$x = 1$

3) $9(1) - 8y = -7$ *Plug in value of x*

4) $9 - 8y = -7$

$-8y = -16$ *Solve for y*

$y = 2$

$(1,2)$ *Final answer*

55. **Answer: B**

We need to isolate z so we can first add x^2 on both sides.

Add x^2 on both sides: $x^2 + \frac{2}{y} = 4z - 24$

Add 24 on both sides: $x^2 + \frac{2}{y} + 24 = 4z$

Multiply $\frac{1}{4}$ on both sides: $\frac{x^2}{4} + \frac{2}{4y} + \frac{24}{4} = z$

Simplify: $\frac{x^2}{4} + \frac{1}{2y} + 6 = z$

Practice Test #6 Answers

1. **Answer: 12**

   This is a permutation problem and since the order can be anything, the permutation of 4 is just 4 * 3.

2. **Answer: 50 square units**

   We one that the longer side is twice as large as the shorter in this rectangle, we also know that the shorter side is 10. If the longer size is twice as much, that means it's 20.

   Since 10 x 2 = 20

   The shaded region is a triangle to find the area of triangle we use formula $(\frac{1}{2} Base \ x \ Height)$.

   We know the height which is 10.

   The base of the triangle is side DC. and we know the midpoint is E making side EC which is the base of the triangle . A midpoint cuts a line in half making side EC = 10

   Plug in our values into the formula and solve $(\frac{1}{2} Base \ x \ Height)$.

   $$\frac{1}{2} 10 \ x \ 10 = \ 5 \ x \ 10 \ = \ 50$$

3. **Answer: 6**

   The repeating decimal $.384615384615$ starts repeating after 5. The repetition contains 6 numbers. 22 divided by 6 is 3 with a remainder of 4. The 4th number in the repeating decimal is 6.

4. **Answer: 112 square inches**

   First, we have to find the total area of the rectangle. We multiply the base and height, 10 * 16, or 160 inches. Then we find the area of the trapezoid. The formula for the area of a trapezoid is $\frac{length\ of\ base\ a + length\ of\ base\ b}{2} * height$. We know that 8 is one of the bases, and so is 16 because opposing sides on a rectangle have the same length measure. Because the shaded section below the trapezoid is 6 inches tall and the total measure of that side is 10, we can subtract 10 and 6 to find the height of the trapezoid, which is four.

   Now, we can find out the area of the trapezoid:

   $\frac{8+16}{2} * 4$, which will give us 48 square inches.

   Finally, because we're only finding the area of the shaded area, we subtract the total rectangle area and the area of the trapezoid, which will give us 112 square inches.

5. **Answer: 11**

   First, we need to find the missing angle. Because 45 and 99 are part of the same triangle, we can use the equation 45+99+y=180 to find the missing angle, which gives us 36 degrees. Now, we can look at the bigger triangle. Because the small triangle and the big triangle share the same angle (36 degrees), we now know 36 and 88 are both angles in the big triangle. We can use the equation 36+88+45+x=180 to find x, giving us x=11.

6. **Answer: C**

   We first distribute the right side of the equation, giving us $24 + 8n = 40n + 64 + 8n$. Combining the like terms gives us $24 + 8n = 48n + 64$. We can then subtract $8n$ and 64 from both sides, giving us $-40 = 40n$. Dividing both sides by 40 gives us our final answer of $n = -1$.

7. **Answer: D**

The equation that represents the problem is $x(x + 2) \times 6 = 288$. First, divide 6 on both sides of the equation. Then distribute the x to (x+2) to get $x^2 + 2x$. Then subtract 48 from both sides of the equation. Then, solve for $x^2 + 2x - 48 = 0$. Next, factor $x^2 + 2x - 48$ and x = 6 will be on your solutions.

8. **Answer: C**

Let's convert $\frac{8}{5}$ to a decimal by doing 100 divided by 5 and multiplying by 8 and moving decimals two places to the left. $\frac{8}{5}$ as a decimal is equal to 1.6 .40% of 1.6 is equal to 1.6 x .4 = .64.

9. **Answer: B**

The distance formula will help us determine which point is closest to the origin: $\sqrt{(x_2 - x_1)^2 + (y_2 - y_1)^2}$. By plugging into the distance formula, we can make $x_1 = 3, x_2 = -7, y_1 = 4.$ and $y_2 = -2$. The distance formula is now $\sqrt{-11^2 + -6^2} = \sqrt{100 + 36} = \sqrt{136}$.

10. **Answer: D**

Divide both sides of the inequality by 7 and *the inequality will be* $x + 6 \leq 8$. Then subtract both sides of the inequality by 6 and the inequality will now be x ≤ 2.

11. **Answer: C**

The surface area can be measured by 2(wl + hl + hw). Plug 45 as w, 110 as h, and 94 as l into the expression. The surface area will be 35,940cm squared and to convert it to square meters, you need to divide it by 10000.

12. **Answer: B**

   1) $43.45k - 63.8 = 5.8(k + 7.9) - 9.6k$

   $43.45k - 63.8 = 5.8k + 45.82 - 9.6k$ *Distribute*

   2) $43.45k - 63.8 = -3.8k + 45.82$ *Combine like terms*

   3) $43.45k = -3.8k + 109.62$

   $47.25k = 109.62$ *Isolate variable*

   4) $k = 2.32$ *Final answer*

13. **Answer: A**

First, we find Patrick's rate in terms of hours. We multipliy 0.075 by 60 (that is the amount of minutes in one hour) and we get 4.5. This means Patrick runs 4.5 miles per hour. Then, we find how long it takes each person to run the race.

9 divided by 4.5 is 2. This means Patrick finishes the race in 2 hours.

9 divided by 3 is 3. This means Neil finishes the race in 3 hours.

We now subtract 3 and 2. This means there is a 1 hour difference between how long they take to finish the race.

14. **Answer: D**

The chance of a coin landing on tails is $\frac{1}{2}$. To find the probability of the coin landing four times, we just need to multiply $\frac{1}{2}$ by itself four times.

15. **Answer: D**

Because Face B has an area of 65 sq cm, we can divide 65 by 5 cm, which is one of the side measures used to calculate the area of Face B, and we get 13.

Face A and Face B both share 13 as a side length, so we can now divide 195 by 13 to find the last side length, giving us 15. 15 is the longest side length and 5 is the shortest side length. 15:5, when simplified is 3:1.

16. **Answer: B**

    We must first find the prime factorization of each number.

    12: 2^2 * 3
    14: 2 * 7
    21: 3 * 7

    For each unique factor, we find where it appears the most and write it that many times.

    This would be 2^2 * 3 * 7. Multiplying this gives us the least common multiple of 84.

17. **Answer: A**

    There are two ways to solve this question. The algebraic way is to multiply both sides of the equation by n, giving us $65 = 0.0065n$. Then, we divide both sides of the equation by 0.0065 to get the final answer of 10,000. The second way to solve this is to first look at the equation. We see that the numerator 65, divided by the variable n, is equal to 0.0065. As the value of both is similar, only offset from each other by factors of 10, we can count the displacement in value. The value is shifted by 4 decimal places, therefore it is a change of 10^4. Thus, our answer is 10^4, which is equal to $10,000$.

18. **Answer: C**

    We can set up a system of equations to solve this problem. Assume a is the number of adults attending the restaurant and c is the number of children attending the restaurant:

    $$a + c = 48 \qquad \text{(this is the total number of people that night)}$$

    $$30a + 15c = 1245 \qquad \text{(this is the total amount of money made that night)}$$

    First, we can find the number of adults that attended the restaurant that night. We can find the amount of adults in terms of the amount of children at the restaurant: $c = 48 - a$.

    Substitute $(48 - a)$ for c: $30a + 15(48 - a) = 1245$

    Distribute: $30a + 720 - 15a = 1245$

    Simplify: $15a + 720 = 1245$

    Subtract: $15a = 525$

    Divide: $a = 35$

    There were 35 adults that attended the restaurant. Find the number of children by subtracting 35 from 48 and we get 13. There were 35 adults and 13 children that night.

19. **Answer: D**

    Each yard is equal to 3 feet. In order to find how much inches a foot on the map is, you divide four by 3, which gives you 4/3 inches or $1\frac{1}{3}$ inches.

20. **Answer: C**

$$1)\ 2n = 6(n - 9) \qquad\qquad\qquad \textit{Cross-multiply}$$

$$2)\ 2n = 6n - 54$$

$$-4n = -54 \qquad\qquad\qquad\qquad \textit{Solve for n}$$

$$n = \frac{-54}{-4}$$

$$n = \frac{27}{2}$$

$$n = 13\frac{1}{2}$$

$$n = 13.5 \qquad\qquad\qquad\qquad\qquad \textit{Final answer}$$

21. **Answer: A**

The first step is to cross-multiply the equation, giving us $0.33y = 0.231$. We then divide both sides of the equation by 0.33, giving us our final answer of $y = 0.7$.

22. **Answer: D**

Since angles HOK and JOL are vertically opposite angles, they are equal to each other. As a result, $44 = 3x + 2$ and we just need to solve for x. Subtract two from both sides of the equation and then divide both sides by 3. x equals 14. 14 x 2 = 28.

23. **Answer: B**

An expression to represent this can x + (x + 1) = 145, which simplifies to 2x + 1 = 145. To solve for x, subtract one from both sides of the equation. Next, divide both sides of the equation by 2 and x is the smallest value of the consecutive integers which is equal to 72.

24. **Answer: B**

1) $25\% = \frac{25}{100}$ *Rewrite percentage as fraction*

2) $\frac{25/25}{100/25} = \frac{1}{4}$ *Simplify fraction*

3) $\frac{1}{4} * 220$

$\frac{220}{4}$ *Multiply*

55 *Final answer*

25. **Answer: B**

We first find the area of the piece of fabric. Because it is a rectangle, we can multiply its base and height, giving us 192 square inches.

Then we find the circle's area, $r^2\pi$ or $r^2 * 3.14$ because we are replacing pi. Replace the variable with the given values: $4^2 * 3.14$ or 50.24 square inches. Because Shirley is cutting OUT the circle, we need to subtract the area of the circle from the area of the fabric: 192 - 50.24=141.76 square inches.

26. **Answer: B**

This expression is equivalent to $\frac{2^6}{2^7}$ which equals 2^{-1} which can be simplified to $\frac{1}{2}$, which is equal to 0.5.

27. **Answer: B**

    1) $40 \ km/h * x \ hours = 60 \ km/h * 2 \ hours$ *Set equation*

    2) $40x = 60 * 2$

    $40x = 120$ *Solve for x*

    $x = 3$ *Final answer*

28. **Answer: B**

    The three angles above all add up to $180°$. We can find x using the equation:$(x + 12) + (4x - 13) + (3x - 3) = 180$. Now, we can solve for x:

    Combine like terms: $(8x - 4) = 180$

    Add 4 on each side: $8x = 184$

    Divide 8 on each side: $x = 23$

29. **Answer: D**

    Before we can isolate b, we can distribute 3a and -1.

    Distribute: $3a^2 + 6a - b + 1 = 64$

    Now we can isolate b.

    Add b to each side: $3a^2 + 6a + 1 = 64 + b$

    Subtract 1 on each side: $3a^2 + 6a = 64 + b - 1$ OR $3a^2 + 6a = 63 + b$

    Subtract 63 on each side: $3a^2 + 6a - 63 = b$

30. **Answer: A**

   1) $-7 - 2x = 3y$ *Rewrite equation to match other equation*

   2) $-3(-21) + -3(-4x) = -3(-y)$ *Multiply equation by -3*
   $63 + 12x = 3y$

   $-7 - 2x = 63 + 12x$ *Both expressions equal 3y*

   3) $-7 = 63 + 14x$
   $-70 = 14x$ *Solve for x*
   $x = -5$

   4) $-21 - 4(-5) = -y$ *Plug variable in to equation*

   5) $-21 - -20 = -y$
   $-21 + 20 = -y$
   $-1 = -y$ *Solve for y*
   $y = 1$

   $(-5, 1)$ *Final answer*

31. **Answer: C**

   The shaded region is a Circle to find the area of the circle we use the formula (πr^2). All we need to do is find the radius, if we know that one of the sides of the square is 10, that makes the diameter of the circle 10 which we know that half of the diameter is the radius of a circle. Half of 10 is 5, making the radius of the circle 5.

   Plug in the 5 to the equation   > $\pi 5^2$
   Simplify   > $\pi 25$ or 25π

32. **Answer: A**

   The chance of picking a red is $\frac{1}{4}$ and the chance of picking a blue is $\frac{1}{5}$. In order to find the probability of getting a red first and then a blue second, we just need to multiply the probability of getting red and blue

33. **Answer: A**

   To solve for x, use inverse operations to isolate it. Multiply 7 on both sides of the equation and our equation will now be 8x + 4 = 84. Next, subtract 4 on both sides of the equation and our equation will be 8x = 80. Finally, divide both sides of the equation by 8. X is equal to 10.

34. **Answer: C**

   We first convert the 1.5 gallons into cups. Because there are 16 cups in a gallon, we can multiply 16 by 1.5, or 24 cups. This is the initial amount of juice before anybody drinks it.

   Billy drinks 4 cups of juice, so we subtract 4 from 24 the total, giving us 20. Sandra drinks 10% of what's left, so we multiply 10% by 20, the new total after Billy drinks his share. We get 2, the number of cups Sandra drinks. We subtract 2 from 20, giving us 18 cups, our final total.

   Alternatively, we can multiply 90% by 20, which would give us 18 cups left in the jug.

35. **Answer: B**

A common denominator for ½ and ⅓ would be 6. Convert ½ to have a denominator of 6 by multiplying the numerator and denominator by 3 to get $\frac{3}{6}$ and convert ⅓ to have a denominator of 6 by multiplying the numerator and denominator by 2 to get $\frac{2}{6}$. By following the rules of PEMDAS, we would do $\frac{3}{6} - \frac{2}{6}$ since it is inside the parentheses. Next, multiply $\frac{1}{6}$ by 2 so it is inside the brackets. After all the parentheses/brackets are gone, exponents is next. $(⅓)^2 = \frac{1}{9}$. Finally, multiplying $\frac{1}{9}$ by 4 is equal to $\frac{4}{9}$.

36. **Answer: B**

We are given the value of y which we must use to solve for x. Therefore, our first is to plug in the value of $y = -2$ into the equation. This gives us $\frac{-94+x}{16} = 5(-2) + 2$. Simplifying the right side of the equation gives us $\frac{-94+x}{16} = -10 + 2$, or $\frac{-94+x}{16} = -8$. Multiplying both sides of the equation by 16 gives us $-94 + x = 16(-8)$. This is equal to $-94 + x = -128$. Adding 94 to both sides of the equation gives us our final answer of $x = -34$.

37. **Answer: B**

To solve, we must first find the prime factorization of each number

     85: 5, 17

     170: 2, 5, 17

     374: 2, 11, 17

We then take every common factor between all numbers, in this case only 17. This gives us our answer of 17.

38. **Answer: B**

∠1 is a supplementary angle to ∠6, because ∠1 and ∠5 are equal to each other. Because supplementary angles when added equal to 180, we can solve for x: $(\frac{3}{4}x + 16) + (2x - 34) = 180$, or x=72. ∠6 and ∠3 equal to each other so ∠3 equals to $2(72) - 34$, or 110 degrees.

39. **Answer: C**

Four times a number indicates we will multiply it by 4, giving us 4x. A number plus 25 means we are going to add 25 to a variable, so we add + 25. And lastly, more indicates the answer will include a greater than sign.

40. **Answer: D**

Midpoint is found by $((\frac{x_1+x_2}{2}), (\frac{y_2+y_1}{2}))$ We plug the values into the formula $((\frac{25+41}{2}),(\frac{42+54}{2})) = (33,48)$.

41. **Answer: D**

1) $\frac{-11}{a-2} = \frac{4}{5}$ *Distribute negative sign*

2) $5(-11) = 4(a - 2)$ *Cross-multiply*

3) $-55 = 4a - 8$

$-47 = 4a$ *Solve for a*

$a = -\frac{47}{4}$

$a = -11\frac{3}{4}$

$a = -11.75$ *Final answer*

42. **Answer: D**

First, we need to isolate b.

Add 3 to both sides: $\frac{7}{8}a + 3 = 14b$

Divide 14 on both sides: $\frac{7}{112}a + \frac{3}{14} = b$ or $\frac{1}{16}a + \frac{3}{14} = b$

43. **Answer: B**

42 divided by 7 is 6. Out of our possible multiple choice answers, B is the only one that is divisible by 6.

44. **Answer: B**

The formula of the perimeter of a circle, or the circumference of a circle, is $2\pi r$, or $2 * 3.14 * r$. The formula of the diameter of a circle is 2r. Because we know the diameter is 24.4, we can rewrite the circumference formula as $24.4 * 3.14$, or 76.30 feet.

45. **Answer: D**

Because there are 100 centimeters in 1 meter, 1.524 converted to centimeters is 152.4.

Then we divide 152.4 by 5 because we are trying to determine how many centimeters is in one foot. We get 30.48.

46. **Answer: D**

$\sqrt{28}$ is equivalent to $2\sqrt{7}$. $(2\sqrt{7})^3$ is equivalent to $2^3 \times \sqrt{7}^3$. This can be simplified as $8 \times 7 \times \sqrt{7}$.

47. **Answer: C**

A can is in the shape of a cylinder, so we should use the volume formula of a cylinder to find the volume of the can, $r^2\pi h$, or $r^2 * 3.14 * h$ once we have replaced the pi. We know the diameter of the can is 5, so we divide it by 2 to find the radius. Now we can replace the variables with the new values: $2.5^2 * 3.14 * 5$ or 98.125 cubic inches.

48. **Answer: B**

In choice A: $3^2 + 4$ *is equal to* 13 not 14. In choice C, 3 - 2 is equal to 1, not 2. In choice D, |3-7| * 4 is equal to 16 not - 16. As a result, choice B is the correct answer.

49. **Answer: B**

1) $(40\ km/h * 4\ hours) + (50\ km/h * x\ hours) = 360\ km$　　　*Set equation*

2) $(40 * 4) + 50x = 360$

$160 + 50x = 360$

$50x = 200$　　　*Solve for x*

$x = 4$ hours　　　*Final answer*

50. **Answer: B**

Slope can be found using the formula: $\frac{y_2-y_1}{x_2-x_1} = \frac{5-(-6)}{-6-5} = \frac{11}{-11} = -1$. The slope for these two points is -1.

51. **Answer: C**

    The sum of the interior angles in a triangle is 180 degrees. By using this information, we can set up the equation as $34 + 78 + c = 180$. Subtract 111 from both sides of the equation and $c = 68$.

52. **Answer: C**

    We can rewrite this problem into an inequality: $20 + 3.5x \leq 41$. Now, we can solve for x.

    Subtract 20 from both sides: $3.5x \leq 21$

    Divide 3.5 on both sides: $x \leq 6$

    Because the sign is greater than OR equal to, the maximum amount of hours he can rent the truck for is 6 hours.

53. **Answer: C**

    1) $365 / 2 = 182.5$ *Find the amount of days in half a year*

    2) $182.5 / 15$ *Divide the number of days by the frequency*

    3) $12.166....$ *Round down*

    12 *Final answer*

54. **Answer: A**

    We have to isolate x.

    Add 15 on each side: $3x = 2y + 15$

    Divide 3 on both sides: $x = \frac{2}{3}y + 5$

    Now, we can multiply by 3 to find the value of 3x.

    Multiply: $3x = 3(\frac{2}{3}y + 5)$

    Distribute: 3x=2y+15

55. **Answer: A**

The average American would be able to fill one heavy duty trash bag to 50% in one day. Since 6 hours is ¼ of the day, they can only fill ¼ of 50% which is 12.5% of the bag.

Practice Test #7 Answers:

1. **Answer: 60**

   First, we need to find out how much mg is in one prescription. We multiply 60 by 4, and we get a total of 240 mg per prescription. If each dose is 12 mg, there are 20 doses in each prescription. If the prescription can be refilled twice, we multiply 20 by 3 for a total of 3 prescriptions, and we get a total of 60 doses in 3 prescriptions.

2. **Answer: 3**

   We can multiply $\frac{c-8}{2} + \frac{d+6}{3} = -3$ by 4 so both equations share 2c:

   Multiply by four: $(\frac{c-8}{2} + \frac{d+6}{3} = -3)\,4 =$

   Distribute: $(\frac{4c-32}{2} + \frac{4d+24}{3} = -12) =$

   Simplify: $(2c - 16 + \frac{4}{3}d + 8 = -12) =$

   Simplify: $(2c - 8 + \frac{4}{3}d = -12)$

   Add 8 on each side: $(2c + \frac{4}{3}d = -4)$

   Now, we can cancel the two equations out.

   $$2c + \frac{4}{3}d = -4$$

   $$- (2c - 6d = -26) \qquad \textit{Note: we can convert 6d into } \frac{18}{3}d.$$

   $$\frac{22}{3}d = 22 \text{ OR } d=3$$

3. **Answer: 8**

We can first multiply both sides of the equation by *2*, which gives us $2(x - 4) = x$. Distributing the left side of the equation gives us $2x - 8 = x$. We can then subtract *2x* from both sides of the equation, giving us $-8 = -x$. Dividing both sides of the equation by *– 1* gives us our final answer of $x = 8$.

4. **Answer: 13**

The median of a set is the number in the middle. Each set has *7* numbers. We arrange the sets in numerical order and find that set A's median is *20* and set B's median is *33*. We subtract *20* from *33* and we get *13*.

5. **Answer: 16**

The shape is a square meaning all sides are equal.

Side BD is 8cm. G is the midpoint of side BD making side BG half of side BD and same with side GD also half of side BD. 8cm / 2 = 4 cm. Side BG and side GD are 4 cm each. We just found 1 side for both triangles.

Side AB is 8cm. E is the midpoint of side AB making side AE half of side AB and same with side EB also half of side AB. 8cm / 2 = 4 cm. Side AE and side EB are 4 cm each. We just found the 2nd side for the 1 st triangle (EBG).

Side CD is 8cm. F is the midpoint of side CD making side CF half of side AD and same with side FG also half of side CD. 8cm / 2 = 4 cm. Side CF and side FD are 4 cm each. We just found the 2nd side for the 2nd triangle (FDG).

Area of triangle formula ($\frac{1}{2} Base \ x \ Height$)

Triangle EBG the sides EB=4 cm and BG=4 cm making the area of that triangle $\frac{1}{2}$ x 4 x 4 = 8 sq cm.

Triangle FDG the sides FD=4 cm and GD=4 cm making the area of that triangle $\frac{1}{2}$ x 4 x 4 = 8 sq cm.

Combine both areas

8 sq cm + 8 sq cm = 16 Sq cm.

6. **Answer: B**

    1) $5(p-5) = 9p$ *Cross-multiply*

    2) $5p - 25 = 9p$

    $-25 = 4p$ *Solve for p*

    $p = -\dfrac{25}{4}$

    $p = -6\dfrac{1}{4}$

    $p = -6.25$ *Final answer.*

7. **Answer: B**

0.625 as a fraction is $\frac{5}{8}$. The reciprocal of $\frac{5}{8}$ is $\frac{8}{5}$. The reciprocal of $\frac{1}{2}$ will be $\frac{2}{1}$, or $\frac{10}{5}$.

$\frac{10}{5} - \frac{8}{5} = \frac{2}{5}$. The reciprocal of $\frac{2}{5}$ will be $\frac{5}{2}$.

8. **Answer: B**

The formula of a rectangular pyramid is $\dfrac{lwh}{3}$. Replacing the variables with the given numbers, we have $\dfrac{5*6*h}{3} = 80$ or $\dfrac{30*h}{3} = 80$. We can multiply 3 on each side and get $30 * h = 240$. We then divide 30 on each side, giving us 8.

9. **Answer: C**

The equation can be set up as x + (x+2) + (x+4)= 45. First, we add like terms which would simplify the equation into 3x + 6 = 45. Next, subtract 6 from both sides of the equation. Finally, divide 3 on both sides of the equation to get x = 13. The next two consecutive odd integers are 15 and 17. The product of 13 and 17 is 221.

10. **Answer: B**

Before we can find the amount of miles Jon ran, we need to find how many miles Adrian runs in terms of x. If Adrian "runs 3 miles less than half of Omar's amount of miles" and Omar runs 3x+14 miles, Adrian must have ran $\frac{3x+14}{2} - 3$ miles. Now that we know how much Omar and Adrian ran, we can find how much they ran combined.

Add Omar and Adrian's miles: $(3x + 14) + (\frac{3x+14}{2} - 3)$

Since we can't add $\frac{3x+14}{2}$ on its own, we can split it up into $\frac{3x}{2}$ and $\frac{14}{2}$ (or 7, when simplified). Now, we can combine like terms.

Split up the fraction: $\frac{6x}{2} + 14 + \frac{3x}{2} + 7 - 3$ *(3x can also be written as $\frac{6x}{2}$.)*

Combine like terms: $\frac{9x}{2} + 18$

11. **Answer: B**

By following the rules of PEMDAS, we first apply exponents so $(.02)^2 = .0004.$, then we multiply to -5 and 0.02 to get -0.1. Finally, we find the sum of .002 and 4.91.

12. **Answer: C**

When 4056 is divided by 22, the quotient will be 184 and a remainder. When 4056 is divided by 23, the quotient will be 176 and a remainder. However, when 4056 is divided by 24, there will be no remainder.

13. **Answer: B**

   1) $2kg = 2(2.2lb)$

   $2kg = 4.4lb$ *Convert to pounds*

   2) $20lb + 4.4lb$ *Add weights*

   $24.4lb$ *Final answer*

14. **Answer: C**

   We must first simplify the numerator of the first fraction. This can be done in two ways: one can solve the parentheses first, to get $\frac{5(8)}{8} + \frac{17}{32}$, then multiplying $5 * 8$ in the numerator to get $\frac{40}{8} + \frac{17}{32}$. One can also use the distributive property of multiplication, multiplying $5 * 5$ and $5 * 3$ to get $\frac{25+15}{8} + \frac{17}{32}$, then adding the two products together to get the same expression: $\frac{40}{8} + \frac{17}{32}$. We must then add the fractions together, which can be done only with a common denominator. To do this, we can multiply both the numerator and denominator of the fraction on the left by 4, giving us a common denominator of 32 and an expression of $\frac{160}{32} + \frac{17}{32}$. Adding these together gives us our final value of $\frac{177}{32}$.

15. **Answer: A**

   We know that triangle XYZ is an isosceles right triangle. We know one of the angle measures must be 90 degrees, so half of 90 must be the angle measure of angle y and angle z, giving us 45 degrees. Now that we know what angle y is equal to, we can find what a is using $\frac{1}{3}a + 12 = 45$, giving us a=99.

16. **Answer: D**

$\frac{17}{4}$ is equal to -4.25 and $-\frac{22}{7}$ is approximately -3.14. The only number that would fit into the inequality is -4.

17. **Answer: B**

We are given the value of y that we must use to solve for n. We thus must plug in the value of $y = 6$ into the equation. This gives us $\frac{9}{2n} = \frac{3(6)}{8}$. This simplifies to $\frac{9}{2n} = \frac{18}{8}$. We can cross-multiply the equation, giving us $36n = 72$. Dividing both sides by 36 yields the final answer of $n = 2$.

18. **Answer: B**

We must first find the prime factorization of each number.

5: 5
12: 2^2 * 3
27: 3^3

For each unique factor, we find where it appears the most and write it that many times.

This would be 2^2 * 3^3 * 5. Multiplying this gives us the least common multiple of 540.

19. **Answer: A**

The area of triangle is $\frac{bh}{2}$ and the area of a circle is $\frac{r^2\pi}{2}$. The radius of the semicircle is 4, because 8 is the diameter of the circle. Replace with the given values, and we have:

Area of triangle: $\frac{8*6}{2}$ or 24

Area of a semicircle: $\frac{4^2\pi}{2}$ or $\frac{16*3.14}{2}$ or 25.12

20. **Answer: D**

We can multiply $6x - 4y = 6$ by 2 so both equations share 8y:

$$(6x - 4y = 6)\ 2 = 12x - 8y = 12$$

Now, we can cancel the two equations out.

$$4x + 8y = -4$$

$$+\ (12x - 8y = 12)$$

—————————————

$$16x = 8 \text{ OR } x = \frac{1}{2}$$

Now that we know x, we can find y. We can replace $\frac{1}{2}$ with x in one of the equations and solve for y:

Replace x with $\frac{1}{2}$: $6(\frac{1}{2}) - 4y = 6$

Multiply: $3 - 4y = 6$

Subtract 3 on both sides: $-4y = 3$

Divide -4 on both sides: $y = -\frac{3}{4}$

We now know that $x = \frac{1}{2}$ and $y = -\frac{3}{4}$, so we divide $\frac{1}{2}$ by $-\frac{3}{4}$, giving us $\frac{5}{4}$.

21. **Answer: A**

First, we distribute the left side of the equation, giving us $14x + 16 = -39 + 3x$. Subtracting $3x$ and 16 from both sides gives us $11x = -55$. Dividing both sides by 11 gives us our final answer of $x = -5$.

22. **Answer: B**

The ratio of red to black to blue is 8:7:5. The proportion of black marbles is $\frac{28}{80}$. After three black pens are moved, the chance of getting a black pen is now decreased to $\frac{25}{75}$ or $\frac{1}{3}$.

23. **Answer: B**

Parallel means the slope needs to be the same. First, we need to isolate y by dividing both sides of the equation by 2 and our equation will now be y = 2x + 4. The slope is 2, which is the same for 4y = 8x + 9

24. **Answer: C**

1) $8\ gallon * \frac{4\ quart}{1\ gallon}$ *Set conversion expression*

$$\frac{8 * 4\ gallon\ quart}{gallon}$$

2) $\frac{8*4\ quart}{1}$ *Cancel out units*

3) $8 * 4\ quart$ *Simplify*

$32\ quarts$ *Total number of quarts*

Each flask holds 1 quart

$32\ quart\ /\ 1\ quart = 32$ flasks

32 flasks   *Final answer*

25. **Answer: D**

$$\left(\frac{8^3 \times 8^{12}}{8^3}\right)^2 = \frac{(8^3 \times 8^{12})^2}{(8^3)^2} = \frac{8^{30}}{8^6} = 8^{24}$$

26. **Answer: D**

To find the length of the shorter side, use the expression x + (x+1) = 19. Combine like terms and our equation is now 2x + 1 = 19. After subtracting one from both sides of the equation and then dividing both sides of the equation by 2, x is equal to 9 which is the length of the shorter side. As a result, the longer side must be 10. 2(9) + 2(10) is 38 which is the perimeter of the rectangle.

27. **Answer: D**

You can find 250% of 120 by multiplying 120 and 2.5. The product of 120 and 2.5 is 300.

28. **Answer: B**

To find the surface area, we use the formula 2(l*h+l*w+w*h). We have a height of 5, a length of 3, and a width of 4. We plug in the values to get 2(3*5+3*4+5*4), and we get a final result of 94 square units.

29. **Answer: A**

We need to isolate a.

Subtract 64 on both sides: $2a^2 = b - 64$

Divide 2 on both sides: $a^2 = \frac{b-64}{2}$

Simplify: $a^2 = \frac{1}{2}b - 32$

Find the square root of each side: $a = \sqrt{\frac{b}{2} - 32}$

30. Answer: B

The equation can be set up as $\frac{x + (x+2) + (x+4) + (x+6) + (x+8)}{5} = 11$. To isolate x, we multiply both sides of the equation by 5. Our equation is now x + (x+2) + (x+4) + (x+6) + (x+8) = 55. We combine like terms and get 5x + 20 = 55. Next, we subtract 20 from both sides of the equation and the equation is now 5x = 35. Finally, we divide both sides of the equation by 5 to get x= 7. The consecutive odd integers are 7, 9 , 11, 13, and 15. 11 is the middle number.

31. Answer: A

1) $(45 \, km/h \, * \, 4 \, hours) \, + \, (70 \, km/h \, * \, x \, hours) \, = \, 320 \, km$ *Set equation*

2) $(45 * 4) + (70x) = 320$

$180 + 70x = 320$

$70x = 140$ *Solve for x*

$x = 2$ hours   *Final answer*

32. Answer: D

To find the slope of the original line, we first need to add 5x to both sides to isolate the y value. Then, we divide both sides by 8 to get just y. Now that we know our slope is 5/8, we need to find a perpendicular slope. To find a perpendicular slope, we take the negative reciprocal of the original slope. The negative reciprocal of 5/8 is -8/5, which is our final answer.

33. **Answer: B**

We can first simplify the right side of the equation by distribution. This gives us $\sqrt{x^3} - 12 = 10 + 1 + 12 - 27$. Combining the like terms yields us $\sqrt{x^3} - 12 = -4$ We can then add 12 to both sides to get $\sqrt{x^3} = 8$. Squaring both sides gives us $x^3 = 64$. Finally, taking the cube root of both sides yields our final answer of $x = 4$.

34. **Answer: C**

The perimeter is the value of all sides, and in the triangle the sides that are given to us are 6 and 8. We must use the Pythagorean theorem to get the hypotenuse, so we do $6^2 + 8^2$, which gives us 100. We get the square root 100, which is 10 and the hypotenuse is 10. To get the perimeter, we add up all the sides, which is 6+8+10, and get a final answer of 24 cm^2

35. **Answer: A**

1) $\frac{2(9)}{\sqrt{36}} / \frac{2}{9}$

$\frac{18}{\sqrt{36}} / \frac{2}{9}$

$\frac{18}{6} / \frac{2}{9}$ *Simplify the fraction using multiplication and square root*

2) $\frac{18}{6} * \frac{9}{2}$ *Divide by fraction: Multiply by reciprocal*

3) $\frac{18*9}{6*2}$

$\frac{162}{12}$ *Multiply numerators and denominators*

4) $\frac{162 \div 6}{12 \div 6}$ *Simplify using greatest common factor (GCF = 6)*

$\frac{27}{2}$ *Final answer.*

36. **Answer: D**

1) $2L * 1/2$ *Find amount of water before spill*

$1L$

2) $1L - 60\% * 1L$ *Subtract amount spilled from amount of water*

$1L - \dfrac{6}{10}L$

3) $\dfrac{4}{10}L$ *Convert to decimal*

$0.4L$ *Final answer*

37. **Answer: B**

Mode is the most frequent number that occurs. If we want to find the mode of the petals, we would look for the highest amount of flowers that had a specific amount of petals. We see that 20 flowers had 5 petals which means that 5 is the mode. Even though only 14 flowers had 12 petals it wouldn't be the answer because most flowers had 5 petals and that makes it the mode. The mode is the number of similar numbers occurring.

38. **Answer: B**

½ is equal to .5 and ⅓ is equal to .666 . The only value that is between .5 and .666 is .55.

39. **Answer: A**

   First, we have to find what the value of b is. To that, we must isolate b.

   Multiply 2 on both sides: $2a = 4b - 5$

   Add 5 on both sides: $2a + 5 = 4b$

   Divide 4 on both sides: $\frac{2a+5}{4} = b$

   Now, we can find what 3b is.

   Multiply both sides by 3: $\frac{6a+15}{4} = 3b$

   Expand the fraction: $\frac{6a}{4} + \frac{15}{4} = 3b$

   Simplify: $\frac{3a}{2} + \frac{15}{4} = 3b$

40. **Answer: A**

   The area of a parallelogram is base * height. Because we know the base length, which is 20cm, we can divide that by the area, giving us 11, meaning 11 is the measure of the height. Because AB+BC must equal to the height, or 11, we can rewrite that as

$$2(x - 3) + (x + 2) = 11$$
$$2x - 6 + (x + 2) = 11$$
$$3x - 4 = 11$$
$$3x = 15$$
$$x = 5$$

41. **Answer: B**

   Since x and y would represent a point that is horizontal and vertically away correspondingly, we can use the Pythagorean theorem to calculate the distance. If it is 5 units away, the distance would be 25. $x^2 + y^2 = c^2$ would help represent our distance for points. For choice A, $(3 - 2)^2 + (5 - 2)^2 = 10$. For choice B, $(5 - 2)^2 + (6 - 2)^2 = 25$.

   For choice C, $(6 - 2)^2 + (2 - 2)^2 = 16$. For choice D, $(4 - 2)^2 + (4 - 2)^2 = 16$.

42. **Answer: A**

To find the price of an item after it is 30% off is the same as multiplying the original price by .7. 500 x .7 = 350. After the customer uses the $10 off coupon, computer A costs 340. Computer B after the 40% sale can be found by multiplying the original price by .6. 600 x .6 = 360. Since 340 is less than 360, it is cheaper and by $20.

43. **Answer: A**

1) $20\,mph * x\,hours = 24\,mph * 5\,hours$

                                   Set equation

2) $20x = 24 * 5$

$20x = 120$ *Solve for x*

$x = 6$ hours   *Final answer*

44. **Answer: C**

We can first simplify the absolute values on the left side of the equation. This gives us $x - |-27| + |-99| = 28$. This can be rewritten as $x - 27 + 99 = 28$. Combining the like terms gives us $x + 72 = 28$. Subtracting 72 from both sides of the equation gives us our final answer of $x = -44$.

45. **Answer: B**

We know that 10% of teens like caramel flavored ice cream and we also know that is 20,000 people. To find how many teens like chocolate we would need to see the percentage of chocolate and set up a proportion.

$\frac{20,000}{10\%} = \frac{x}{45\%}$ cross multiply > 20,000 x (45) = 10x > simplify and solve > x = 90000

That means 90,000 teens like chocolate flavored ice cream.

46. **Answer: D**

Each interior angle of an octagon is 135 degrees. An exterior angle is 180 subtracted by the interior angle. 180-135=45.

47. **Answer: D**

Plug in what y is equal to in the equation and the equation will be 2x + 4x + 3 = 33. Next, combine like terms resulting in 6x = 30. Finally, divide both sides of the equation by 5. As a result, x will equal 5.

48. **Answer: A**

Convert $\frac{74}{12}$ to a mixed number which should be $6\frac{2}{12}$. $6\frac{2}{12}$ is between 6 and 7.

49. **Answer: B**

To solve, we must first find the prime factorization of each number.

66: 2, 3, 11

84: 2, 2, 3, 7

We then take every common factor between all numbers, in this case 2 and 3, and multiply them. This gives us our answer of 6.

50. **Answer: D**

First, we need to isolate a:

Subtract 2b on both sides: $8a + 3c = 180 - 2b$

Subtract 3c on both sides: $8a = 180 - 2b - 3c$

Divide 8 on both sides: $a = \frac{180 - 2b - 3c}{8}$

Split up the fraction: $a = \frac{180}{8} - \frac{2b}{8} - \frac{3c}{8}$

Simplify: $a = \frac{45}{4} - \frac{1}{4}b - \frac{3}{8}c$

51. **Answer: A**

   $\sqrt{72}$ can be simplified to $6\sqrt{2}$ and $\sqrt{48}$ can be simplified to $4\sqrt{3}$. $6\sqrt{2} - 4\sqrt{3}$ can't be simplified.

52. **Answer: B**

   First you need to know that x+2 and y+3 are both the radius of the quarter circle. The radius in a circle is always the same , meaning that x+2 is equal to y+3. We need to find y in terms of x, or simply isolate the y.

   -Set up the equation > $x + 2 = y + 3$

   -Subtract 3 from both sides > $x - 1 = y$

   And we get y by itself , and y in terms of x equals x-1.

53. **Answer: B**

   1) $5 * 12 + 6$ *Convert feet and inches to inches*

   $60 + 6$

   $66\ in.$

   2) $66\ in * \frac{2.54\ cm}{1\ inch}$ *Set conversion expression*

   $\frac{66 * 2.54\ in\ cm}{1\ in}$

   3) $66 * 2.54 cm$ *Cancel out units*

   4) $167.64 cm$ *Simplify*

   5) $184 - 167.64 cm$ *Subtract heights*

   $16.36 cm$ *Final answer*

54. **Answer: C**

    We first simplify the left side of the equation by using the distributive property of multiplication. This gives us $28 - 12x - 5 + x = 5x - 5$. We can then combine like terms to get $23 - 11x = 5x - 5$. We can then add $11x$ and 5 to both sides of the equation, giving us $28 = 16x$. Dividing both sides of the equation by 6 gives us our final answer of $x = \frac{28}{16}$, which simplifies to $x = \frac{7}{4}$.

55. **Answer: A**

    Let x = the number of candies Henry consumed. 3x - 10 equals the number of candies Eric consumed. Since Eric ate 30 candies, 3x - 3 = 30. Add 3 to both sides of the equation and the equation is now 3x = 33. Divide both sides of the equation by 3 and x is equal to 11.

Practice Test #8 Answers:

1. **Answer: 200**

   Since x is equal to 20, half of x is 10, ¼ of 20 is 5, and ⅕ of 20 is 4. As a result, the height is 10, the width is 5, and the length is 4. The volume can be found by the products of 10,5, and 4.

2. **Answer: 83**

   By applying the rules of PEMDAS, you use the exponent first as a $|-4|^3 = 64$. Then you do multiplication of ¼ and 4 which gives you 1. Finally, you add all 64 + 4 + 1 + 14 and the sum will be 83.

3. **Answer: 275**

   2^5 is equivalent to 2 * 2 * 2 * 2 * 2 = 32 and 3^5 is equivalent ot 243 and the sum of 32 and 243 is 275.

4. **Answer: 124**

    We can solve this problem by splitting the shape into two: a triangle and a rectangle, like this:

    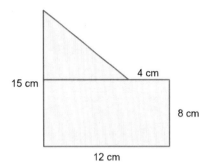

    We know the sides of the rectangle are 12 and 8. We can find the area by multiplying them together, giving us 96 square centimeters.

    Then we need to find the base and height of the triangle. We know the total side length of the triangle and the rectangle is 15, so we can subtract the side length of the rectangle, which is 8, giving us 7 centimeters. This is the height of the triangle.

    Next, we must find the base of the triangle. We know the length of the rectangle, which is 12, and we also know the length of space is not part of the triangle base, 4. We can subtract these two numbers to give us the base length of the triangle, 8 centimeters.

    Now, we can find the area of the triangle, $\frac{base * height}{2}$, or $\frac{8*7}{2}$, or 28 square centimeters. Then we can add the area of the rectangle and the area of the triangle together, 28+96, or 124 square centimeters.

5. **Answer: 10**

    The first number that is a multiple of 6 in the set is 42. We find the difference between the largest number in the set and the first number which is a multiple of 6. 100 - 42 = 58. Then divide 58 by 6 and around 9.8 but we need to round it down. 9 + 1(from the 42) = 10.

6. **Answer: B**

   1) $42\,mph * x\,hours = 70\,mph * (x-2)\,hours$

   Set equation

   2) $42x = 70(x-2)$

   $42x = 70x - 140$

   $-28x = -140$ *Solve for x*

   $x = 5$ hours   *Final answer*

7. **Answer: A**

   Probability is represented as part being the numerator and total as the denominator. The total is calculated as the sum of 2,4,3, and 1 which is 10. If he doesn't choose white, there are six other hoodies he has so that would be represented as $\frac{6}{10}$.

8. **Answer: D**

   To solve this, we simply find the prime factorization of 56, being 2 * 2 * 2 * 7, or 2^3 * 7 in exponential form.

9. **Answer: A**

   We first must distribute the left side of the equation. This gives us $2x + 10 + 5x = 4x + 1$. Combining like terms yields $7x + 10 = 4x + 1$. Subtracting $3x$ and 10 from both sides of the equation gives us $3x = -9$. Dividing both sides by 3 brings us to our final answer of $x = -3$.

10. **Answer: D**

We know that 2 of the kids got 60. Additionally, we know everyone else got 100. If there were 5 students, and we know the scores of 2 students, that means that 3 other students got 100. Therefore, the test scores may be 60, 60, 100, 100,100. To find the mean we simply add all the test scores $60 + 60 + 100 + 100 + 100 = 420$

Now divide by how many students there are which is 5

$420 \div 5 = 84$

11. **Answer: D**

1) $\left|\frac{2}{3} - \frac{9}{6}\right| * \frac{35}{13}$ *Convert mixed number to improper fraction*

2) $\left|\frac{2*2}{3*2} - \frac{9}{6}\right| * \frac{35}{13}$

$\left|\frac{4}{6} - \frac{9}{6}\right| * \frac{35}{13}$ *Subtract fractions in absolute value. (LCM = 6)*

3) $\left|\frac{-5}{6}\right| * \frac{35}{13}$

$\frac{5}{6} * \frac{35}{13}$ *Solve absolute value*

4) $\frac{5*35}{6*13}$ *Multiply fractions*

$\frac{175}{78}$ *Already in simplest form, final answer.*

12. **Answer: A**

The racetrack is 6 miles long. Since Ariana wants to finish the racetrack in 30 minutes, she needs to go 6 miles in 30 minutes. This can be represented by the equation 6=1/2x. Multiply both sides by 2 and x, which is the speed that Ariana needs to go at, is equal to 12 miles per hour.

13. **Answer: C**

Because the pentagon is regular, all the angles are the same. The total angle measure of a pentagon is 540 degrees. To find the angle measure of one side, we divide by 5 (which is the number of angles inside the pentagon), giving us 108. We then have to find the supplementary angle: 180-108=72. Now we can multiply by five, because a, b, c, d and e equal to each other. This gives us 360 degrees.

14. **Answer: C**

One bill is equal to 30 coins. Since we want to find out how many coins 48 bills equal, we multiply 48 and 30, and we get a total of 1440 coins.

15. **Answer: D**

The radical rule states that $\frac{\sqrt{96}}{\sqrt{48}} = \sqrt{\frac{96}{48}}$ which is equivalent to $\sqrt{2}$.

16. **Answer: B**

1) $\frac{3}{17} \div \frac{2}{5} * \left(\frac{24}{4} + \frac{5*2}{2*2}\right)$

$\frac{3}{17} \div \frac{2}{5} * \left(\frac{24}{4} + \frac{10}{4}\right)$

$\frac{3}{17} \div \frac{2}{5} * \frac{34}{4}$ *Add fractions in parentheses*

2) $\frac{3}{17} * \frac{5}{2} * \frac{34}{4}$ *Divide fractions: PEMDAS = Multiply/Divide left-to-right*

3) $\frac{3*5*34}{17*2*4}$

$\frac{510}{136}$ Multiply numerators/denominators together

4) $\frac{510 \div 34}{136 \div 34}$ *Simplify using greatest common factor (GCF = 34)*

5) $\frac{15}{4}$ *Final answer.*

17. **Answer: D**

To find the slope of the two points, we use the formula y_2-y_1 divided by x_2-x_1. We fill in the values, resulting in (8-(-4)) / (-2-10), which gives us a slope of -1.

18. **Answer: C**

Ryan's starting amount is 750. After spending $100 on the gift, he has $650. Once he puts 10% into the savings account, 650(.9) = 585.

19. **Answer: D**

First, we need to isolate x.

Distribute 5: $-15 + 10x + 4x = y$
Combine like terms: $-15 + 14x = y$
Add 15 on both sides: $14x = y + 15$
Divide 14 on both sides: $x = \frac{1}{14}y + \frac{15}{14}$

20. **Answer: B**

We can set up the equation as x(x+2) = 288. First, distribute the x to (x+2) to get $x^2 + 2x$. Then subtract 288 from both sides of the equation. Then solve for $x^2 + 2x - 288 = 0$. Next, factor $x^2 + 2x - 288$, and x = 16 will be one of your solutions. The even number after 16 is 18.

21. **Answer: A**

A pentagon has an interior angle of 108 and an equilateral triangle has an interior angle of 60. We then find their exterior angle, which is the 180 minus the interior angle giving us 72 degrees for the pentagon and 120 for the triangle. 120-72= 48.

22. **Answer: C**

1) $5(n - 3) = 8(5n - 4)$ *Cross-multiply*
2) $5n - 15 = 40n - 32$
$-15 = 35n - 32$
$17 = 35n$ *Solve for n*
$n = \frac{17}{35}$ *Can't be simplified, final answer*

3. **Answer: C**

We know that the mean is 18. Meaning that all numbers that are presented added and then divided by how many there are should give us 18.

This could be represented with an equation $(14 + 15 + 23 + 13 + 22 + x) \div 6 = 18$

Simplify: $(87 + x) \div 6 = 18$ $>$ $\frac{87+x}{6} = 18$

Cross multiply: $18(6) = 87 + x$ $>$ $108 = 87 + x$

Subtract 87 from both sides to isolate the x $21 = x$

24. **Answer: B**

1) $-6x + 72 = 3x$ Distribute

2) $72 = 9x$ Isolate variable

$x = 8$ Final answer

25. **Answer: B**

We must first find the prime factorization of each number.

20: 2^2 * 5
56: 2^3 * 7

For each unique factor, we find where it appears the most and write it that many times.

This would be 2^3 * 5 * 7. Multiplying this gives us the least common multiple of 280.

26. **Answer: B**

The repeating pattern in the repeating decimal contains 5 digits: 1,4,9,6, and 3. 33 divided by 5 is 6 with a remainder of 3. We use the remainder value to find which number we use in the repeating pattern. The 33rd number in our pattern is 9.

27. **Answer: A**

To find the area of this figure, we have to first split up the figure into two parts, a triangle and a square. To find the area of the square, we do *length * width*, and we get an area of 64 square inches. To find the area of the triangle, we first need to find the sides. The base of the triangle includes 2 inches, 8 inches, and 2 inches, so we add 2+8+2, and the base is 12 inches. The height of the triangle is 14 minus the 8 inches from the square, and the height is 6 inches. The area of a triangle is ½ * *base * height*, and when we multiply the ½ * 12 * 8, we get 36 square inches. Finally, we add 36 square inches and 64 square inches to get a final answer of 100 square inches.

28. **Answer: D**

$$11)\ 4.3b + 36.55 - 5.1(b - 9.9) = 86.88$$
$$4.3b + 36.55 - 5.1b + 504.9 = 86.88 \qquad\qquad \textit{Distribute}$$

$$2) - 0.8b + 36.55 + 50.49 = 86.88$$
$$-0.8b + 87.04 = 86.88 \qquad\qquad \textit{Combine like terms}$$

$$3) - 0.8b =- 0.16 \qquad\qquad \textit{Isolate variable}$$

$$b = 0.2 \qquad\qquad \textit{Final answer}$$

29. **Answer: C**

The total number of people Jaden served is 30. There are 14 students with 2 siblings and one student with 3 or more siblings. $\frac{14}{30} + \frac{1}{30} = \frac{15}{30}$.

30. **Answer: C**

Less indicates subtraction, 6 less would mean -6 . The word less than indicated that we are subtracting with that number. Product means multiply , product of x and z would essentially mean   x times z   or   xz

Combine the two terms 6 less (- 6....)   and product of x and z (....xz) $-6 +$ xz or $xz - 6$

31. **Answer: C**

1) $12 = 12x - 24y$ *Rearrange elements of equation*

2) $-6(-7x) + -6(4y) = -6(-27)$
$42x - 24y = 162$ *Multiply equation by 6*

$-24y = 162 - 42x$
$-24y = 12 - 12x$ *Isolate y of both equations*

$12 - 12x = 162 - 42x$ *Both expressions equal to - 24y*

3) $12 + 30x = 162$
$30x = 150$ *Solve for x*
$x = 5$

4) $-7(5) + 4y = -27$ *Plug variable in to equation*

5) $-35 + 4y = -27$
$4y = 8$ *Solve for y*
$y = 2$

$(5,2)$ *Final answer*

32. **Answer: D**

The numbers that are written include 4,14,24,34, 40, 41, 42, 43, 44, 45, 46,47, 48 and 49. There are 14 numbers but 44 has two "4", it counts as 2.

33. **Answer: B**

First, multiply both sides of the inequality by 3. Next, subtract 5 from both sides of the inequality Finally, divide both sides of the inequality by 2. The inequality is now x > 29.

34. **Answer: D**

A right angle is 90 degrees. We can write the equation as 38 + 2x + 6 = 90 and solve for x. First, we combine like terms and our equation would now be 2x + 44 = 90. Subtract 44 from both sides of the equation and then divide by 2. x equals 23. 2 x 23 = 46.

35. **Answer: A**

1) $12\,fl.oz * \dfrac{1L}{33.8\,fl.oz}$ — Set conversion expression

$\dfrac{12\,fl.oz\,L}{33.8\,fl.oz}$

2) $\dfrac{12\,L}{33.8}$ — Cancel out units

3) $12/33.8\,L$ — Simplify

$0.36L$ — Final answer

36. **Answer: B**

Use the equation: x + (x+2) + (x+4) = 90. Once you combine like terms, the equation is 3x + 6 = 90. After subtracting 3 on both sides of the equation, 3x = 84. Divide both sides of the equation by 3 and x is equal to 28, which is the shortest side.

37. **Answer: C**

To find which number set has the highest mode we first need to find modes of each set.

> *Set A* [14,15,15,16,16,16,17,18,19,19]: 16 is the mode since it gets repeated the most often.
>
> *Set B* [15,15,15,15,17,17,18,19,19,20]: 15 is the mode since it gets repeated the most often.
>
> *Set C* [16,16,17,17,18,18,18,19,19,20]: 18 is the mode since it gets repeated the most often.
>
> *Set D* [16,16,16,16,21,21,23,24,25,28]: 16 is the mode since it gets repeated the most often.

Looking at all these values we can see 18 is the highest mode and Set C has that mode.

38. **Answer: D**

The total amount has to be a multiple of 6 since when you find the probability of it being green , it has to be a whole number.. A,B, and C are not multiples of 6.

39. **Answer: B**

Triangle ABC has a total area of 70 sq units. We are also given the area of two other triangles inside 12 sq units and 36 sq units. To find the area of triangle DCE we would need to set up an equation like so.

$$12 \text{ sq units } + \text{ } 36 \text{ sq units } + \text{ } Area \text{ } of \text{ } DCE \text{ } = \text{ } 70 \text{ sq units}$$
$$48 \text{ sq units } + \text{ } Area \text{ } of \text{ } DCE = 70 \text{ sq units}$$

Subtract 48 from both sides > $Area \text{ } of \text{ } DCE = 22 \text{ sq units}$

40. **Answer: B**

First simplify the expression using the distributive property in which the equation would look like 3x - 15 -10x + 45 = 22. Next, combine like terms so the equation is now -7x +30 = 22. Then, subtract 30 from both sides of the equation, -7x = -8. Finally, divide both sides of the equation by -7. x = $\frac{8}{7}$

41. **Answer: A**

1) $\frac{8}{n+2} = \frac{-12}{7}$ *Distribute negative*

2) $8(7) = -12(n+2)$ *Cross-multiply*

3) $56 = -12n - 24$
$80 = -12n$ *Solve for n*
$n = -\frac{80}{12}$
$n = -\frac{20}{3}$
$n = -6\frac{2}{3}$
$n = -6.67$ *Final answer*

42. **Answer: A**

Since Pete is running around the field, we know that this question has to do with perimeter. To find the perimeter of the field, we add up the given dimensions, which are 10 yards and 30 yards. Our equation should look like 2(10+30), which will give us an answer of 80 yards total. Considering that Pete runs 10 yards per minute, we divide 80 yards by 10 yards to get 8 minutes.

43. **Answer: A**

By using prime factorization, we know that 525 is 5 * 5 * 5 * 5. This is equivalent to $(5^4)^2 = 5^8$.

44. **Answer: D**

We have to isolate a.

> *Divide c on both sides:* $-4a - 2b = \frac{36}{c}$
>
> *Add 4a on both sides:* $-2b = \frac{36}{c} + 4a$
>
> *Divide -2 from both sides of the equation:* $b = \frac{\frac{36}{c}+4a}{-2}$
>
> *Simplify:* $b = \frac{36}{c} * \frac{1}{-2} + 4a * \frac{1}{-2}$ or $b = -\frac{18}{c} - 2a$

45. **Answer: B**

The perimeter of a rectangle can be found by using the formula: 2l + 2w which l stands for length and w stands for width. If the length is 6, then the width is 18. 2(6) + 2(18) = 48.

46. **Answer: D**

Shawn's pace is 9/4 mph and Emma's pace is 17/5 mph. 9/4 * 6 is 27/2 and 17/5 * 6 is 102/5. 102/5 - 27/2 is 69/10, which is 6.9 in decimal form.

47. **Answer: B**

Half of a number minus five is represented as ½ x - 5. Since it is less, we use the less than sign. Five times the difference of 20 and a number is represented as 5(20-x).

48. **Answer: C**

To find 5x+7 we first need to find x .

If x+3 = 9, to get x we would need to isolate it by subtracting 3 from both sides and get x=6

Plug in the x=6 for 5x+7   > 5(6) + 7 = 30+7 = 37

49. **Answer: D**

    P is located at -1, and Q is located at 9. The midpoint of PQ is calculated through the sum of -1 and 9 and then divide that sum by 2. -1 + 9 = 8 and 8 divided by 2 is 4.

50. **Answer: A**

    1) $150\ lb * \frac{1\ kg}{2.2\ lb}$ *Set conversion expression*

    $\frac{150\ lb\ kg}{2.2\ lb}$

    2) $\frac{150\ kg}{2.2}$ *Cancel out units*

    3) $150\ /\ 2.2\ kg$
    $68.1818...kg$ *Package weight converted*

    4) $68.181818...kg\ /\ 2kg$ *Divide weights*
    $34.09...kg$ *Round down*

    34 bricks   *Final answer*

51. **Answer: D**

    A 40% discount is the same as multiplying the original price by .6. So $360 is 60% of the original price. We can find the original price by using the equation .6x = 360 where x represents the original price. x is found by dividing both sides of the equation by .6 and then x = 600.

52. **Answer: B**

    We first must simplify the right side of the equation. This gives us $x + 2 = \frac{16-3}{5}$. This is equal to $x + 2 = \frac{13}{5}$. Subtracting 2 from both sides gives us $x = \frac{13}{5} - 2$. Rewriting 2 as a fraction allows us to subtract the like terms. This gives us $x = \frac{13}{5} - \frac{10}{5}$. Simplifying this yields the final answer of $x = \frac{3}{5}$.

53. **Answer: D**

There are 200 numbers in that range. If a number is divided by 2 and 3, then the number has to be divisible by 6. 200 divided by 6 is equal to 33.333 repeating. 33.333 rounded down is 33.

54. **Answer: B**

The area for a circle is found with the formula $A = r^2\pi$. Once we plug in the values, the equation will be $49\pi = r^2\pi$. Next, divide both sides by π. $49 = r^2$ and the square root of 49 is 7 so r equals 7. Circumference is found by multiplying radius by 2π. $7 \times 2\pi = 14\pi$.

55. **Answer: A**

1) $8(a - 5) = 10a$ *Cross-multiply*

2) $8a - 40 = 10a$
$-40 = 2a$ *Solve for a*

$-20 = a$ *Final answer*

Practice Test #9 Answers:

1. **Answer: 82**

   First, find the total score of the people by multiplying 76 (The mean) by 5 (The number of people taking the test,) which will give 380 as the total score. Then find Ed's score by subtracting everyone's score (72,69, 82, 75) from 380. That will result in Ed's score, which is 82 points.

2. **Answer: 103**

   Because the numbers are consecutive and odd, first set the five consecutive numbers as x, x+2, x+4, x+6, and x+8. Then set up an equation to the problem x+2 + x+4 + x+6 + x+8 = 495, when simplified, the equation will be 5x + 20 = 495. We then simplified further as the problem will be 5x = 475. X is then solved by dividing 5 from both sides, as x = 95. To find the largest odd number, substitute 95 as x in x+8, which will get 95+8 = 103 as the final answer.

3. **Answer: 250**

   Subtract 64% from 100%, which gives 36% of the people that prefer buses over cars. Then divide 90 by 36% to get 100% of the people, which will be 250.

4. **Answer: 240**

   First we set Rose's weight as x. Then we set Johnny's weight as 2x, as he is twice of Rose's weight. Then we set Mary's weight as 4x, as she is twice of 2x (Johnny's weight.) We then proceed the solution by forming an equation, which will be x + 2x + 4x = 840. As all of their weights were up 840 pounds. We then simplify the problem down to 7x = 840, and solve for x by dividing 7 from both sides. This will result in Rose's weight, or x, as 120. We then substitute x for 120 and solve for Johnny' weight by multiplying 120 by 2, giving 240 as the final answer.

5. **Answer: 360**

   Each small square has a side of 6. We need to find the base and height of the triangle to find the area of the figure.

   We can see that the base of the triangle stretches out into 4 squares, since each square is 6. Multiply 4 x 6 to get the value of the base which is 24.

   Same with the height of the figure which stretches out to 5 squares, and 5 x 6 = 30. This means the height is 30.

   To find the area of the triangle we use the formula $(\frac{1}{2} Base \ x \ Height)$

   -Plug in our values   > $\frac{1}{2} 24 \ x \ 30$

   -Simplify and Solve   > $12 \ x \ 30 = 360$

6. **Answer: A**

   Starting out, the chance of getting a pink higher is ⅛. Once you remove 3 pink highlighters and add 5 yellow highlighters, there are only 5 pink highlighters and 26 highlighters in total.

7. **Answer: C**

1) $\frac{2}{5} * \frac{7}{2} - \frac{4}{3} / \frac{7}{3}$ *Convert mixed numbers to improper fractions*

2) $\frac{2*7}{5*2} - \frac{4}{3} / \frac{7}{3}$

$\frac{14}{10} - \frac{4}{3} / \frac{7}{3}$ *Multiply numerators and denominators of fractions*

3) $\frac{14}{10} - \frac{4}{3} * \frac{3}{7}$ *Divide fractions: Multiply by reciprocal*

4) $\frac{14}{10} - \frac{4*3}{3*7}$

$\frac{14}{10} - \frac{12}{21}$ *Multiply numerators and denominators of fractions*

5) $\frac{14*21}{10*21} - \frac{12*10}{21*10}$

$\frac{294}{210} - \frac{120}{210}$

$\frac{174}{210}$ *Subtract using common denominator (LCM = 210)*

6) $\frac{174 \div 6}{210 \div 6}$ *Simplify using greatest common factor (GCF = 6)*

$\frac{29}{35}$ *Final answer.*

8. **Answer: B**

We can first simplify the numerator of the right side of the equation. The cube root of 8 is 2, so our equation becomes $\frac{2}{6} = \frac{2+n}{3}$. Cross-multiplying gives us $6 = 6(2+n)$. Distributing the right side of the equation gives us $6 = 12 + 6n$. Subtracting 12 from both sides of the equation gives us $6n = -6$. Dividing both sides of the equation by 6 gives us our final answer, $n = -1$.

9. **Answer: C**

   1) $-4(x) +-4(-\frac{5}{2}y) =-4(-\frac{3}{2})$

   $-4x + 10y = 6$ *Multiply equation by -4*

   2) $10y = 14 - 4x$ *Isolate y of both equations*

   $10y = 6 + 4x$

   $6 + 4x = 14 - 4x$ *Both expressions equal 10y*

   3) $6 + 8x = 14$

   $8x = 8$ *Solve for x*

   $x = 1$

   4) $10y + 4(1) = 14$ *Plug variable in to equation*

   5) $10y + 4 = 14$

   $10y = 10$ *Solve for y*

   $y = 1$

   $(1,1)$ *Final answer*

10. **Answer: D**

    The equation for the surface area of a cube is $6a^2$. Plug $5x^2$ as a: $6 (5x^2)^2 = 150x^4$

11. **Answer: D**

    The sum of five consecutive integers can be expressed as x + (x+1) + (x+2) + (x+3) + (x+4) which can be simplified to 5x + 10. When we set that expression to each of the options, 5x + 10 = 55 is the only one that results in x being an integer.

12. **Answer: C**

   If a plant grows 86 centimeters in a year and since there are 12 months a year, it grows at a rate of 86/12 per month, and 86 divided by 12 is $7\frac{1}{6}$.

13. **Answer: A**

   We need to isolate x.

   Add 3y on both sides: $5x = 12 + 3y$

   Divide 5 on both sides: $x = \frac{12+3y}{5}$

   Split up the fraction: $x = \frac{3}{5}y + \frac{12}{5}$

14. **Answer: D**

   The slope formula is calculated through the change in y over change in x. The change in y for the two points -4 - (-2), which is -2 and the change in x is calculated through 4 - (-4) which is 8. $\frac{-2}{8} = \frac{-1}{4}$. Choice D is the correct answer.

15. **Answer: B**

   Use the method of FOIL, 3x multiplied by 3x is $9x^2$. 3x multiplied by -y is -3xy. 3x multiplied by 2y is 6xy. Finally, 2y multiplied by -y is $-2y^2$. Once we combine all of these terms, the result would be $9x^2 + 3xy - 2y^2$.

16. **Answer: C**

   The first number that is a multiple of 4 in the set is 204. We find the difference between the largest number in the set and the first number. $250 - 201 = 49$. Then divide 49 by 4 and it is 12.25 but we need to round it down. We get an answer of 12.

17. **Answer: D**

First, we convert the exponents from standard notation to standard form. 0.1×10^2 would be 10 and 100×10^{-2} would be 1. Our new expression is $\frac{9^{10}}{9^1}$. Because we are dividing exponents we subtract the exponents, giving us 9^9.

18. **Answer: C**

Since the probability of choosing a piece of lucky charms at random, is twice as great as the probability of choosing a piece of cheerios, then the amount of cheerios is 4. $\frac{part}{total} = \frac{4}{15}$.

19. **Answer: D**

1) $|-3-4| + 4^2 * 12 - 8$

$|-3-4| + 16 * 12 - 8$ *Solve the exponent*

2) $|-3-4| + 16 * 12 - 8$

$|-3-4| + 192 - 8$ *Multiply*

3) $|-3-4| + 192 - 8$ *Solve for absolute value*

$|-7| + 192 - 8$

$7 + 192 - 8$

4) $7 + 192 - 8$ *Add/Subtract*

191

191   *Final answer*

20. **Answer: B**

We can solve this by figuring out how much weight the garden wagon can hold with the 86 pounds of cement on it. Subtract 86 from 345, the maximum weight, to get the amount of weight left the garden wagon can hold. We get a result of 259 pounds remaining. We divide 259 pounds by 5, which is the weight of one brick, and get 51.8. We round down to our final answer of 51 bricks.

21. **Answer: A**

   We know that each cubic cm contains 2 tennis balls. Since we are asked how many tennis balls there are in total, we would need to know how many cubic cm the box is.

   To find that we will need to use the formula to find the volume of a rectangular prism, which is: (*Width x Length x Height*)

   We are given all of these dimensions:

   Width = 10 cm   Length = 5 cm   Height = 3 cm

   Plug in the values for the equation and solve:

   $10\ cm \times 5\ cm \times 3\ cm\ =\ 150\ cm^3$

   We know the volume of the whole box, since each cubic cm contains 2 tennis balls we would need to multiply the total amount of cubic centimeters by the amount of balls in each cubic cm.

   $$150\ cm^3 x\ \frac{2\ tennis\ balls}{cm^3} = 300\ \text{tennis balls}$$

22. **Answer: D**

1) $\frac{7 \, km}{1 \, hr} * \frac{1 \, hr}{60 \, min} * \frac{1000 \, m}{1 \, km} * \frac{3.28 \, ft}{1 \, m}$ *Set conversion expression*

$$\frac{7 * 1000 * 3.28 \; km \; hr \; m \; ft}{60 \; hr \; min \; km \; m}$$

2) $\frac{7 * 1000 * 3.28 \, ft}{60 \, min}$ *Cancel out units*

3) $7000 * 3.28 / 60 \, ft/min$

$22960 / 60 \, ft/min$ *Simplify*

$382.66... \, ft/min$ *Speed of driver*

4) $\frac{382.66 \, ft}{1 \, min} = \frac{4280 \, ft}{x}$ *Set proportion*

5) $382.66x = 4280$ *Cross-multiply*

$x = 11.184$

$11.18 \, minutes$ *Final answer*

23. **Answer: C**

We can set up a proportion to find how much flour is used to make 117 cups of flour: $\frac{4}{9} = \frac{x}{117}$. We can simplify 9 and 117, giving us $\frac{4}{1} = \frac{x}{13}$. Cross multiply and solve for x and we get x=52. This is the amount of flour used to make one project's worth of paper mache. Since we need 3 of these projects, we multiply 52 by 3, giving us 156 cups of flour.

24. **Answer: B**

In order to find what 2a-3 is equal to, we need to find what a is equal to first. We need to isolate a first.

Subtract 3b on each side: $-2ab = 12 - 3b$

Divide -2b on each side: $a = \frac{12-3b}{-2b}$ OR $\frac{3b-12}{2b}$

Now, we can substitute a as $\frac{3b-12}{2b}$ in 2a-3.

Substitute: $2(\frac{3b-12}{2b}) - 3$

Distribute: $\frac{3b-12}{b} - 3$

Split the fraction up: $\frac{3b}{b} - \frac{12}{b} - 3$

Simplify: $3 - 3 - \frac{12}{b}$

Combine like terms: $-\frac{12}{b}$

25. **Answer: C**

$1000\% = \frac{1000}{100} = 10$ *Convert percentage to fraction*

$5278 * 10 = 52780$ *Multiply*

26. **Answer: A**

To find x^4, we need to isolate x. We are given that z=64 and $y^6 = z$. If we substitute 64 for z, we get $y^6 = 64$. Take the 6th root of both sides to get y by itself and we get 2.

If $2x = y$ and $y = 2$, we can substitute 2 for y into the equation $2x = y$, giving us $2x = 2$. Now, we can find what x is equal to. Divide 2 on both sides to isolate x and we get x=1.

Raise the 1 to the fourth power and find x^4.

$$1^4 = 1$$

27. **Answer: B**

First, we need to isolate b.

Square both sides: $2b = a^2 - 6a + 9$ (Use FOIL.)

Divide both sides by 2: $b = \frac{a^2-6a+9}{2}$

Split up the fraction: $b = \frac{a^2}{2} - \frac{6a}{2} + \frac{9}{2}$

Simplify: $b = \frac{1}{2}a^2 - 3a + \frac{9}{2}$

28. **Answer: D**

The formula for a square pyramid is $(side\ length)^2 * \frac{height}{3}$. We know what the width and height of the square pyramid is, so our equation will look like:

$$8^2 * \frac{6}{3}$$

$64 * 2 = 128$ cubic inches.

29. **Answer: D**

We can set up the equation as x(x+1)(x+2) = 720. First, we expand the equation by multiplying x , x + 1, and x +2 to get $x^3 + 3x^2 + 2x$. Next, we subtract 720 from both sides of the equation. Our equation should now be $x^3 + 3x^2 + 2x$ - 720 = 0. To find what x is, we need to factor (x-8)$(x^2 - 11x + 90)$ and from this, we know 8 is a possible solution. The consecutive numbers that follow 9 and 10. The sum of 8,9, and 10 is 27.

30. **Answer: C**

Our first step is to use the distributive property to simplify the left side of the equation. This gives us $15 + 6n - 6 + 30n = 9$. Combining the like terms gives us $9 + 36n = 9$. Subtracting 9 from both sides of the equation gives us $36n = 0$. Dividing both sides by 36 gives us our final answer of $n = 0$.

31. **Answer: C**

    1) $3(x - 9) = 8x$ *Cross-multiply*

    2) $3x - 27 = 8x$

    $-27 = 5x$ *Solve for x*

    $x = -\dfrac{27}{5}$

    $x = -5\dfrac{2}{5}$

    $x = -5.4$ *Final answer*

32. **Answer: D**

    To find the difference, we first need to find the mean score. To find the mean, add up all the numbers and divide by how many numbers there are.

    In this case, we have 6 numbers which all add up to 504:

    $(78 + 93 + 84 + 63 + 88 + 98) = 504$

    Now, we need to divide 504 by 6:

    $504 \div 6 = 84$

    The mean score is 84, and Katy's score is 63; the difference between their scores are 21 since $84 - 63 = 21$.

33. **Answer: A**

First, we distribute the 2 in the equation $2(s - 2t) = -20$, giving us $2s - 4t = -20$. Now, our system of equations will look like:

$$2s - 4t = -20$$
$$4s + 3t = 4$$

We then need to multiply/divide the equations so both equations share the same variable and coefficient so we can easily cancel it out. We can do this by multiplying 2 by $2s - 4t = -20$, giving us $4s - 8t = -40$.

Now that both equations have 4s, we can cancel it out:

$$4s - 8t = -40$$
$$- (4s + 3t = 4)$$
$$\text{----------------------}$$
$$-11t = -44 \text{ OR } t=4$$

34. **Answer: B**

Angles 3 and 4 are supplementary angles, which mean they equal 180° combined. Since we have the value for angle 4, we can subtract it from 180° to get the value of angle 3. 180 - 125 = 55, which is our final answer.

35. **Answer: A**

We can first simplify the equation by distribution. This gives us $\frac{n+6}{4+14} = \frac{6n-54}{3^3}$. Simplifying the denominators gives us $\frac{n+6}{18} = \frac{6n-54}{27}$. Cross-multiplying gives us $27(n + 6) = 18(6n - 54)$. Distributing both sides of the equation gives us $27n + 162 = 108n - 972$. Subtracting $108n$ from both sides gives us $-81n + 162 = -972$. We then subtract 162 from both sides which gets us $-81n = 1134$. Dividing both sides by -81 gives us our final answer of $n = -14$.

36. **Answer: C**

The question above relates to permutation since we want to rearrange the items. There are 5 different items, as a result, $5! = 5 \times 4 \times 3 \times 2 \times 1$ which is equal to 120.

37. **Answer: D**

Area of triangle formula ($\frac{1}{2} Base\ x\ Height$)

We are given the height of 8, we need to find the base. The base is the distance between q and p. To find that distance we would need to subtract p from q.

So, Height = 8   Base = $q - p$.

Plug it the formula $\frac{1}{2} Base\ x\ Height$ > $\frac{1}{2}(q - p)\ x\ 8$

Rearrange   > $\frac{1}{2}8\ x\ (q - p)$

Simplify   > $4(q - p)$

38. **Answer: C**

First, we can set up a system of equations. Let c=the number of cupcakes and m=the number of muffins.

$$8c + 5m = 23.75$$

$$4c + 11m = 35.25$$

Now, we can solve. We can multiply $4c + 11m = 35.35$ by 2 so both equations share 8c.

Multiply: $2(4c + 11m = 35.35)$

Distribute: $8c + 22m = 70.70$

Now, we can eliminate c.

$$8c + 5m = 23.75$$

$$-(8c + 22m = 70.50)$$

$$-17m = -46.75 \text{ OR } m=2.75$$

Now we know a muffin costs \$2.75. We can now replace m with 2.25 in one of the equations and solve for c.

Replace: $8c + 5(2.75) = 23.75$

Multiply: $8c + 13.75 = 23.75$

Subtract 11.25 on both sides: $8c = 10$

Divide 8 on both sides: $c = 1.25$

We now know that one cupcake is \$1.25 and one muffin is \$2.75.

We need to find the cost of 3 cupcakes and 2 muffins.

$(3*1.25)+(2*2.75)= 9.25$

39. **Answer: B**

1) $\frac{m+11}{4} = \frac{-10}{6}$ *Distribute negative*

2) $-10(4) = 6(m + 11)$ *Cross-multiply*

3) $-40 = 6m + 66$

$6m = -106$ *Solve for m*

$$m = -\frac{106}{6}$$

$$m = -\frac{53}{3}$$

$$m = -17\frac{2}{3}$$

$m = -17.67$ *Final answer*

40. **Answer: A**

First, we need to find out how fast they travel in minutes. 10 miles per hour = 10 miles per 60 minutes. We divide the entire equation by 60 so ⅙ mile per minute. ½ divided by ⅙ is 3, which gives us an answer of 3 minutes to fall ½ of a mile.

41. **Answer: C**

First, we create an equation. $\frac{a}{5} = 2.05$. Then, multiply both sides by 5 to isolate a. The final answer is 10.25

42. **Answer: B**

   1) $106 = 18a + 18 + 5(9a + 5)$

   $106 = 18a + 18 + 45a + 25$ *Distribute*

   2) $106 = 18a + 45a + 43$

   $106 = 63a + 43$ *Combine like terms*

   3) $63 = 63a$ *Isolate variable*

   $a = 1$ *Final answer*

43. **Answer: A**

   $16 \times 16 = 256, 17 \times 17 = 289, 18 \times 18 = 324$, and $19 \times 19 = 361$. As a result, $\sqrt{324}$ is equal to 18.

44. **Answer: A**

   To find the difference between the amount of people who ate 3 meals and the amount of people that ate 4 meals, we first need to find the amount of people who ate 3 meals and the amount of people that ate 4 meals. Since there is a sample size of 3,200, we multiply 3,200 by the percentages. 48% of people said they ate 3 meals, so we multiply 3,200 by 48%, or 0.48, and get 1536. 12% of people said they ate 4 meals, so we multiply 3,200 by 12%, or 0.12, and get 384. To find the difference, we subtract 1536 - 384, and get 1152.

45. **Answer: B**

   We need to isolate y.

   Subtract $\frac{1}{12}x$ on both sides: $\frac{3}{4} - \frac{1}{12}x = -\frac{3}{8}y$

   Multiply $-\frac{8}{3}$ on both sides: $-\frac{24}{12} + \frac{8}{36}x = y$ OR $-2 + \frac{2}{9}x = y$

46. **Answer: B**

The midpoint can be calculated through $((\frac{x_1+x_2}{2}), (\frac{y_1+y_2}{2}))$. We can solve it by The midpoint can be calculated through $((\frac{-4+x_2}{2}), (\frac{4+y_2}{2})) = (0,2)$. $((\frac{-4+x}{2}) - 0$ when x $= 4, (\frac{4+y_2}{2})) = 2$ if $y = 0$.

47. **Answer: B**

Because 7 is equal to $\sqrt{49}$ and 8 is equal to $\sqrt{64}$, a would be all numbers in between 49 and 64, which are 50,51,52,53,54,55,56,57,58,59,60,61,62,63, which is a total of 14. Because one of the signs is greater than or equal to, we also include 49, which gives us 15.

48. **Answer: C**

1) $572 - \frac{1}{4} * 572$ *Find volume after water removal*

$$572 - 143$$

$429 \, mL$ *Remaining water*

2) $429 \, mL * \frac{1 \, L}{1000 \, mL} * \frac{1.06 \, quart}{1 \, L}$ *Set conversion expression*

$$\frac{429 * 1 * 1.06 \, mL \, L \, quart}{1000 * 1 \, mL \, L}$$

3) $\frac{429 * 1.06 \, quart}{1000}$ *Cancel out units*

4) $454.74 / 1000 \, quart$ *Simplify*

0.45474 *Round down*

$0.45 \, quart$ *Final answer*

49. **Answer: A**

Following the rules of PEMDAS, you do the operations inside the parentheses. As a result, 3- 4 is -1. Then, the operation inside the left bracket is 5 - (-1) = -4. Since there is an absolute value sign, it is 4. 4 - 6 is equal to -2.

50. **Answer: B**

First, we find how many times the ball landed into the basket. To find that we multiply 75 and 0.20, giving us 15. This is the amount of times the ball landed into the basket before she throws the ball 25 more times.

Now, we multiply 25 by 0.2, giving us 5. This is the amount of times the ping pong is predicted to land in the basket.

We add and 20 is our answer.

51. **Answer: D**

The line representing the inequality is an open circle, so we can eliminate choices A and C. The line represents equations $-3 < x < 7$.

Now, we have to solve for x.

First, we can find B by breaking it into two inequalities.

Find the absolute value of B:

$3x - 6 > 15$

Add six on both sides: $3x > 21$

Divide by 3 on both sides: $x > 7$

$3x - 6 < -15$

Add six on both sides: $3x > -9$

Divide by 3 on both sides: $x < -3$

(we switch the signs because we are dividing with a negative number)

So the inequality for B would be $-3 > x > 7$, which does not equal to $-3 < x < 7$. We can eliminate B. D must be the answer.

52. **Answer: C**

The probability of drawing a blue jelly bean is $\frac{32}{80} = \frac{2}{5}$ which is equal to 40%. The probability of drawing a yellow jelly bean is $\frac{20}{80} = \frac{1}{4}$ which is equal to 25%. The difference between 40% and 25% is 15%.

53. **Answer: A**

We can first distribute the left side of the equation which gives us $35x - 28 - 1 = 14 - 6x$. Combining the like terms gives us $35x - 27 = 14 - 6x$. We can then add $8x$ and 27 to get $41x = 41$. Dividing both sides by 41 gives us our final answer of $x = 1$.

54. **Answer: B**

We can solve this question by setting up a proportion. $\frac{3456}{32} = \frac{5000}{x}$. To solve for x, we cross multiply and get 3456x = 160000. Divide both sides by 3456. x=1250/27, or 46.296. Since we can't use part of a bag of flour and if we round down it won't be enough, we round up and get an answer of 47 bags of flour to make 5000 muffins.

55. **Answer: A**

1) (x mph * (2+3) hours) = ((x+30) mph*3 hours)   *Set equation*

2) (2 + 3)x = 3(x + 30)
5x=3x+90
2x=90   *Solve for x*

x=45 mph   *Final answer*

Practice Test #10 Answers:

1. **Answer: 250**

   We are given dimensions of the picture itself which is 10 units wide and 5 units long. Also, we are given the dimensions of the whole picture + frame which is 20 units wide and 15 units long.

   Area of picture is: $10 \times 5 = 50$

   Area of Frame + Area of Picture is $20 \times 15 = 300$

   In order to find just the area of the frame, subtract the two areas.

   Area of Frame = (Area of Frame + Area of Picture) - Area of Picture.

   -Plug in the values   > $(300) - 50$

   -Solve   > 250

2. **Answer: 11**

   Find the remainder from dividing 281 by 15, which will give 11 as an answer.

3. **Answer: 48**

   Find the greatest common factor by listing out all the factors of 192 and 144, then select the largest shared factor, which will be 48.

   An alternative method would be to use prime factorization and multiply all the common prime factors they have together.

4. **Answer: 2**

   We can multiply 5a-b=12 by 3 so both equations share 3b.

   Multiply: $3(5a - b = 12)$

   Distribute: 15a-3b=36

   Now, we can put it into a system of equations:

   $$15a - 3b = 36$$
   $$+(6a + 3b = 6)$$
   $$============$$
   21a=42 OR a=2

5. **Answer: 25**

   First determine the constant rate in the pattern, which is 4. We then use the sequence formula $a_n = a_1 + (n-1)d$, where n is the amount of terms in the sequence. We then substitute the respective values into the formula, $96 = 0 + (n-1)4$. This equation is simplified into $96 = 4n-4$, which is then further simplified into $100 = 4n$. Finally, divide both sides by 4 and the equation will result in $n = 25$, which is the final answer.

6. **Answer: D**

   If a number is divisible by 7 and 9, the number should be divisible by 63. We need to find which number is a multiple of 63 and that would be choice D since 252 divided by 63 is 4.

7. **Answer: D**

   We can first simplify the left side of the equation via distribution. This gives us $-7n - 4 + 8n = -4$. Combining the like terms gives us $-4 + n = -4$. Adding 4 to both sides of the equation gives us our final answer of $n = 0$.

8. **Answer: C**

   We know all sides on a square are equal. And the area of a square is ($Base \times Height$). We are given that the diagonal is 8. Using the pythagorean theorem we set up an equation to find s

   $$8^2 = s^2 + s^2 \quad \text{Simplify} > \quad 64 = 2s^2$$

   To get s by itself divide 2 on both sides

   $$\frac{64}{2} = \frac{2s^2}{2} \quad \text{Simplify} > \quad 32 = s^2$$

   To get rid of the power 2 on the square root both sides

   $$\sqrt{32} = \sqrt{s^2} \quad \text{Simplify} > \quad 4\sqrt{2} = s$$

   We know $4\sqrt{2} = s$

   All that is left is to multiply (s x s) to find area of square

   $$4\sqrt{2} \times 4\sqrt{2} = 32$$

9. **Answer: C**

The reciprocal of ⅖ is $\frac{5}{2}$ and the reciprocal of $\frac{4}{7}$ is $\frac{7}{4}$. The product of $\frac{5}{2}$ and $\frac{7}{4}$ is $\frac{35}{8}$.

$(\frac{35}{8})^2 = \frac{1225}{64} = 19.1$

10. **Answer: D**

First subtract 4 from both sides of the inequalities. The inequality is now $7x > 48 + x$. Next, subtract x from both sides of the inequality. The inequality is now $6x > 48$. Finally, divide both sides of the inequality by 6, which gives us $x > 8$. Since x needs to be greater than 8, the only answer choice remaining is 9.

11. **Answer: C**

In order to find the value of 3a+1, we need to find the value of a. In order to do that we need to isolate a.

Subtract $\frac{1}{2}b$ on both sides: $4a = 24 - \frac{1}{2}b$

Divide 4 on both sides: $a = 6 - \frac{1}{8}b$

Now, we can replace a with $6 - \frac{1}{8}b$ in 3a+1.

Substitute: $3(6 - \frac{1}{8}b) + 1 = 3a + 1$

Distribute 3: $18 - \frac{3}{8}b + 1 = 3a + 1$

Combine like terms: $19 - \frac{3}{8}b = 3a + 1$

12. **Answer: C**

1) $x\ km/h * (2 + 4)\ hours = 75\ km/h * 4\ hours$

Set equation

2) $(2 + 4)x = 75 * 4$

$6x = 300$

Solve for x

$x = 50$

Final answer

13. **Answer: A**

You can set up proportions of $\frac{96}{x} = \frac{12}{100}$, then begin to solve for x. As a result, it would be 9600 = 12x. Divide both sides of the equation by 12, then it would be x = 800.

14. **Answer: A**

1) $\frac{2}{3} + \frac{4}{5} + \frac{5}{4}x = \frac{3*154+1}{60}$ *Distribute values in parentheses*

2) $\frac{2}{3} + \frac{4}{5} + \frac{5}{4}x = \frac{462+1}{60}$

$\frac{2}{3} + \frac{4}{5} + \frac{5}{4}x = \frac{463}{60}$ *Simplify right side of equation*

3) $\frac{4}{5} + \frac{5}{4}x = \frac{463}{60} - \frac{2}{3}$ *Subtract $\frac{2}{3}$ from both sides of equation*

4) $\frac{4}{5} + \frac{5}{4}x = \frac{463}{60} - \frac{2*20}{3*20}$

$\frac{4}{5} + \frac{5}{4}x = \frac{463}{60} - \frac{40}{60}$

$\frac{4}{5} + \frac{5}{4}x = \frac{423}{60}$ *Combine like terms on right side (LCM = 60)*

5) $\frac{5}{4}x = \frac{423}{60} - \frac{4}{5}$ *Subtract $\frac{4}{5}$ from both sides of the equation*

6) $\frac{5}{4}x = \frac{423}{60} - \frac{4*12}{5*12}$

$\frac{5}{4}x = \frac{423}{60} - \frac{48}{60}$

$\frac{5}{4}x = \frac{375}{60}$ *Combine like terms on right side (LCM = 60)*

7) $x = \frac{375}{60} \div \frac{5}{4}$ *Divide both sides of equation by $\frac{5}{4}$*

8) $x = \frac{375}{60} * \frac{4}{5}$ *Divide by fraction: Multiply by reciprocal*

9) $x = \frac{375*4}{60*5}$

$x = \frac{1500}{300}$ *Multiply numerators and denominators*

10) $x = \frac{1500 \div 300}{300 \div 300}$ *Simplify fraction (GCF = 300)*

$x = 5$ *Final answer*

15. **Answer: D**

To find x^3 we would need to find x by itself. We are given that z=16 and $y^2 = z$ if we plug in 16 for z we get $y^2 = 16$ take the square root of both sides to get y by itself and we get $y = 4$

If $x^2 = y$ and $y = 4$ we can plug in 4 for y into the $x^2 = y$ equation.

$x^2 = 4$ take the square root of both sides to get x by itself and you get x=2

Raise the 2 to the third power to find x^3

$$2^3 = 8$$

16. **Answer: C**

The first number that is divisible by 6 in our set is 12. The largest number (54) minus the first number that is divisible by 6, which is 12, is 42. 42 divided by 6 is 7. 7 plus our first number since we include 12 is 8.

17. **Answer: D**

We first need to find b in terms of a.

Subtract 4b on both sides: $-2a = 16 - 4b$

Divide -2a on both sides: $a = -8 + 2b$

Now, we can square a, now that we know what a is in terms of b.

Square: $(2b - 8)^2$

Expand: $(2b - 8)(2b - 8)$

Use FOIL: $(2b)(2b) + (2b)(-8) + (-8)(2b) + (-8)(-8)$

Simplify: $4b^2 - 16b - 16b + 64$

18. **Answer: A**

The formula of the volume of a cube is *side length^3*. So when we replace the variables with our given number, $\sqrt{3}^3$. We can break this up into $\sqrt{3} * \sqrt{3} * \sqrt{3}$. Because $\sqrt{3}*\sqrt{3}=3$, our answer will be $3\sqrt{3}$.

(

19. **Answer: D**

1) $4x - 22.8 = -2.5(1 + 0.8x) + 3.1x$

$4x - 22.8 = -2.5 - 2x + 3.1x$ *Distribute*

2) $4x - 22.8 = -2.5 + 1.1x$ *Combine like terms*

3) $4x = 20.3 + 1.1x$

$2.9x = 20.3$ *Isolate variable*

$x = 7$ *Final answer*

20. **Answer: B**

1) $\dfrac{45 \, mi}{1 \, hr} * \dfrac{5280 \, ft}{1 \, mi} * \dfrac{1 \, hr}{60 \, min} * \dfrac{1 \, min}{60 \, sec}$ *Set conversion expression*

$\dfrac{45 \, mi}{1 \, hr} * \dfrac{5280 \, ft}{1 \, mi} * \dfrac{1 \, hr}{3600 \, sec}$

$\dfrac{45 * 5280 \, mi \, ft \, hr}{3600 \, hr \, mi \, sec}$

2) $\dfrac{45*5280 \, ft}{3600 \, sec}$ *Cancel out units*

3) $237600 / 3600 \, ft/sec$ *Simplify*

$66 \, ft/sec$ *Final answer*

21. **Answer: B**

We must first find the prime factorization of each number.

28: 2^2 * 7

56: 2^3 * 7

98: 2 * 7^2

For each unique factor, we find where it appears the most and write it that many times.

This would be 2^3 * 7^2. Multiplying this gives us the least common multiple of 392.

22. **Answer: C**

An inequality to represent this problem would be 60x ≤ 200.

We divide both sides of the inequality by 60 and the inequality is x ≤ 3.333333.

Since he can't go ⅓ of the times, we have to round down to 3. 3 is the greatest number of times.

23. **Answer: A**

1) $8(x - 1) = 7x$ *Cross-multiply*

2) $8x - 8 = 7x$

$-8 = -x$ *Solve for x*

$8 = x$ *Final answer*

24. **Answer: C**

Because all the slices are identical, we can find the area of one slice and multiply by 4 (not 5, because we are only finding the area of 4 slices). The base of the triangle is 5 m and the height is 4 m. The formula of the area of a triangle is $\frac{base * height}{2}$, so $\frac{20}{2}$ once we have replaced the variables with our given values or 10 square meters. Now we multiply by 4 and we get 40 square meters.

25. **Answer: B**

There are 365 days in a year. In 5 years there are (6 x 365 days) = 2190 days. Alyssa goes to her swimming lessons every 2 days once. Meaning if there are 2190 days and every 2 days she has swimming lessons to find how many days she will go you would divide the two.

$$2190 \div 2 = 1095$$

26. **Answer: C**

1) $3(-7x) + 3(-8y) = 3(-1)$ *Multiply equation by 3*

$$-21x - 24y = -3$$

Solve using elimination

2) $(21x - 21x) + (24y - 24y) = (6 - 3)$ *Add equations*

$$0 + 0 = 3$$

3) $0 \neq 3$ *Variables canceled out*

As both variables are canceled out, and the resulting statement is false, there are no solutions to this system of equations.

27. **Answer: A**

The median is the number in the sequence which is in the middle of all numbers when lined up from lowest to highest.

    A. [27,83,45,67,92] lowest>highest   [27,45,67,83,92] median > 67

    B. [12,12,53,56,99] lowest>highest   [12,12,53,56,99] median > 53

    C. [98,99,25,23,22] lowest>highest   [22,23,25,98,99] median > 25

    D. [109,87,52,13,28] lowest>highest   [13,28,52,87,109] median > 52

Number sequence A has the highest median.

28. **Answer: D**

The numbers from 0 - 20 are for numbers: 2,7,12, and 17. Every number from 20-30 has a 2 so that adds another 10 numbers. In addition to 32 and 37, it would be another 2 numbers. As a result, the sum of 10,4, and 2 is 16.

29. **Answer: C**

We know that the distance between PQ is 7.55. On the number line right is always increasing in value so P has to be smaller in value than Q. That makes answer A automatically wrong. Knowing this is then you just subtract the distance between from where point Q is located to find point P. Point Q is 4.35 so set up an equation 4.35 -7.55 = P and we get P= -3.2.

30. **Answer: B**

Assuming sea level = 0 ft, the initial altitude is -345 ft

Speed of ascension= 475 ft/hr

Time elapsed = 5 hours

Initial altitude + (Speed * Time) = Final altitude

$$-345 + (475 * 5) = 2030$$

2030 ft is the final answer

31. **Answer: A**

Solve using elimination

1) $(6x - 3x) + (-2y + 2y) = (-12 + 9)$

$3x + 0 = -3$ *Add equations*

2) $3x = -3$ *Solve for x*

$x = -1$

3) $-3(-1) + 2y = 9$ *Plug in value of x*

4) $3 + 2y = 9$

$2y = 6$ *Solve for y*

$y = 3$

$(-1,3)$ *Final answer*

32. **Answer: A**

Use Pemdas: Parenthesis, Exponents, Multiplication, Division, Addition, Subtraction.

Solve the parts in the order of operations

33. **Answer: B**

The equation can be set up as x + (x + 1) = 35. which simplifies to 2x + 1 = 35. when we combine like terms. We subtract one on both sides of the equation and our equation should be 2x = 34. Finally, divide both sides of the equation by 2 and x is equal to 17. The next number is 18. 18 divided by 6 is equal to 3.

34. **Answer: B**

The distance formula will help us determine which point is closest to the origin: $\sqrt{(x_2 - x_1)^2 + (y_2 - y_1)^2}$. For choice A, the distance is $\sqrt{89}$. For choice B, the distance is $\sqrt{85}$. For choice C, the distance is $\sqrt{117}$. For choice D, the distance is $\sqrt{98}$.

35. **Answer: D**

First, we convert all our centimeters to meters using the given conversion rate, 1cm = 3m. 15 cm will turn into 45m, 24 cm will turn into 72 m, and 5 cm will turn into 15 m. Now, we need to find the remaining sides that aren't given. 45 - 15 = 30, 72 - 45 = 27. To find the perimeter, we add up all the numbers. 45+45+72+15+27+30=234. Our final answer is 234 meters.

36. **Answer: B**

First, we can isolate x. Because we are solving for the absolute value, we can break this into two inequalities. $30 > |3x - 9|$ can be written as $|3x - 9| < 30$.

$$3x - 9 < 30$$

Add 9 on each side: $3x < 39$

Divide 3 on each side: $x < 13$

$$3x - 9 > -30$$

Add 9 on each side: $3x < -21$

Divide 3 on each side: $x > -7$

(we switch the signs because we are dividing with a negative number)

Now that we know that $-7 < x < 13$, any number (excluding -7 and 13) in between -7 and 13 are equal to x. Choice B is the only answer that is between -7 and 13.

37. **Answer: D**

   1) $3(n - 10) = 2n$ *Cross-multiply*

   2) $3n - 30 = 2n$

   $-30 = -n$ *Solve for n*

   $n = 30$ *Final answer*

38. **Answer: A**

The distance between Asim's house and the grocery store can be written as $y = 3x - 9$. In order to find the total distance, we need to find what $\frac{1}{2}x + 4$ is in terms of y.

   Add 9 on both sides: $y + 9 = 3x$

   Divide 3 on each side: $\frac{y}{3} + 3 = x$

Now, that we know the value of x, we can substitute x in $\frac{1}{2}x + 4$ to find what it is in terms of y.

   Substitute: $\frac{1}{2}(\frac{y}{3} + 3) + 4$

   Distribute: $\frac{1}{2} * \frac{y}{3} + \frac{1}{2} * 3 + 4$

   Simplify: $\frac{y}{6} + \frac{3}{2} + 4$ *(4 can also be written as $\frac{8}{2}$)*

   Combine like terms: $\frac{y}{6} + \frac{11}{2}$

Now that we know what both of the distances are in terms of y, we can add them together.

   Add: $y + \frac{y}{6} + \frac{11}{2}$ *(y can also be written as $\frac{6y}{6}$)*

   Simplify: $\frac{7y}{6} + \frac{11}{2}$

39. **Answer: D**

   1) $6 * 12 + 2$ *Convert feet and inches to inches*

   $72 + 2$

                         74 inches

2) $74\ in * \frac{2.54\ cm}{1\ in}$ *Set conversion expression*

$$\frac{74\ *\ 2.54\ in\ cm}{1\ in}$$

3) $\frac{74\ *\ 2.54\ cm}{1}$ *Cancel out units*

4) $74 * 2.54cm$ *Simplify*

5) 187.96 *Round up*

$188\ cm$ *Final answer*

40. **Answer: C**

The mode is simply how many times a number occurs if 5 is the mode that means that number 5 has occurred more often than any other number, but that doesn't give us any indication as to what the median or the mean could be.

41. **Answer: D**

We know that there are a total of 120 students in this school and 66 are girls. That means that the rest have to be boys. We find boys by subtracting 66 girls from 120 students which is 54 boys. Now to find the percent of boys compared to the whole school we divide 54 boys by the total number of students which is 120.

So $54 \div 120 = 45\%$

42. **Answer: C**

Choices A, and B are not primes numbers since 91 is divisible by 7 and 93 is divisible by 3. Although 97 and 103 are prime numbers, we need the smallest one.

43. **Answer: B**

   We must first simplify the left side of the equation by using the distributive property. This gives us $2x + 34 - 8^2 = 3x$. Simplifying the exponent gives us $2x + 34 - 64 = 3x$. Combining the like terms gives us $2x - 30 = 3x$. Subtracting $2x$ from both sides gives us our final answer of $-30 = x$.

44. **Answer: B**

   We can write the ratio in fraction form and solve for x. $\frac{x}{49} = \frac{3}{7}$. Once we cross multiply we get 7x=147. We divide both sides by 7 and get 21.

45. **Answer: C**

   The formula of the volume of a rectangular prism is $width * length * height$. We use the formula of the volume of a rectangular prism because the piece of metal and the hole both are rectangular prisms.
   Because the side length of the piece of metal is 6 feet, the hole must be 3 feet, because the hole is twice as small.
   We then find the volume of the hole and the volume of the piece of metal if it did not have a hole through it.

   (6*6*12) or 432 cubic feet

   (3*3*12) or 108 cubic feet

   Finally, we subtract the two values from each other. This is because the volume of the piece of metal does not include the hole.

   432-108=324 cubic feet

46. **Answer: C**

   The conversion equation of F to C is $(F - 32) \times \frac{5}{9} = C$. First, we convert 203 F° to Celcius, which would be 95 C°. We then subtract 20 F° from 95 F° to get 75 F°, which is the amount of degrees the pan needs to decrease. We divide 75 by 5 and get 15 hours.

47. **Answer: B**

To find which neighborhood has the most cars we need to find how many cars each neighborhood has.

In neighborhood A, there are 300 cars per car show, there are 10 car shows. Set up an equation to find out how many cars

$$300 \text{ cars per car show} \times 10 \text{ car shows} = 3000 \text{ cars}$$

In neighborhood B there are 300 cars per car show, there are 30 car shows. Set up an equation to find out how many cars

$$300 \text{ cars per car show} \times 30 \text{ car shows} = 9000 \text{ cars}$$

In neighborhood C there are 400 cars per car show, there are 20 car shows. Set up an equation to find out how many cars

$$400 \text{ cars per car show} \times 20 \text{ car shows} = 8000 \text{ cars}$$

In neighborhood D there are 200 cars per car show, there are 40 car shows. Set up an equation to find out how many cars

$$100 \text{ cars per car show} \times 40 \text{ car shows} = 4000 \text{ cars}$$

Compare the cars in each neighborhood, and we can see neighborhood B has the most cars.

48. **Answer: C**

The problem is a combination as a result the formula for this will be $\frac{total\ amount!}{unique\ ones!!} = \frac{7!}{2!\ 2!\ 1!\ 1!\ 1!} = 1260$. Since there are two 2s, two 3s, one 9, one 8, and one 0.

49. **Answer: B**

Since the numerators have that same base, the exponents can be added together and now the numerator will be 12^7. 12^7 can be broken down to $3^7 \times 4^7$. The expressions is now $\frac{3^7 \times 4^7}{4^7}$, we cancel the 4^7 on the numerators and denominator and now our the expressions is just 3^7. 3^7 is equal to 2187.

50. Answer: B

First, we neeed to find the difference between the rates of Glenn and Lola, 8-6.5, or 1.5. This is the distance between the two every hour. We can divide 9 by 1.5 to find the number of hours it takes for Lola to catch up to Glenn. We get 6 hours. Lola takes 6 hours to catch up to Glenn.

51. Answer: A

The equation needs to have a slope of 3 so the coefficient needs to be equal to 3 allowing choice C to be eliminated. After plugging in 2 as the x variable and 8 as the y variable, choice A is the only one that's true.

52. Answer: B

Reciprocal is when you swap the numerator and denominator. After swapping the numerator and denominator, the fraction will be $-\frac{7}{4}$. The product of 2 and $-\frac{7}{4}$ is $-\frac{14}{4}$. 5 converted to a fraction with a common denominator with $-\frac{14}{4}$ is $\frac{100}{20}$. $-\frac{14}{4}$ with a denominator of 20 will make the numerator 70. $-\frac{70}{20} + \frac{100}{20}$ is equal to $\frac{30}{20}$ which is equal to 1.5

53. Answer: D

First, we can distribute both sides of the equation. This gives us $-4 + 4x + 4 = -24 - 8x$. Combining the like terms on the left side gives us $4x = -24 - 8x$. Adding $8x$ to both sides gives us $12x = -24$. Dividing both sides of the equation by 12 gives us $x = -2$, which is our final answer.

54. **Answer: B**

We know that triangle ABC is an isosceles triangle. This means two of its angle measures must be equal to each other. The total angle measure of a triangle has to be 180 degrees, so to find the measure of angle A or C, we can use the equation: 2a+50=180, or 65 degrees. Because angle x and angle c are interior alternate angles, they have to be equal to each other. Therefore, angle x is equal to 65 degrees.

55. **Answer: C**

Convert centimeters to meters

1) $200 \ cm * \dfrac{1 \ m}{100 \ cm}$

$\dfrac{200 \ * \ 1 \ cm \ m}{100 \ cm}$

Set conversion expression

2) $\dfrac{200 \ * \ 1}{100} \ m$

Cancel out units

3) $200 \ / \ 100 \ m$

$2 \ m$

Simplify

Length of rope #2

4) $370 \ cm \ * \dfrac{1 \ m}{100 \ cm}$

$\dfrac{370 \ * \ 1 \ cm \ m}{100 \ cm}$

Set conversion expression

5) $\dfrac{370 \ * \ 1}{100} \ m$

Cancel out units

6) $370 \ / \ 100 \ m$

$3.7 \ m$

Simplify

Length of rope #4

7) $40 \ m + 2 \ m + 16 \ m + 3.7 m$

$61.7 \ m$

Find total length of rope

8) $61.7 \ m * \dfrac{3.28 \ ft}{1 \ m}$

$\dfrac{61.7 \ * \ 3.28 \ m \ ft}{1 \ m}$

Set conversion expression

9) $\dfrac{61.7 \ * \ 3.28 \ ft}{1}$

Cancel out units

10) $61.7 \ * \ 3.28 \ ft$

Simplify

11) $202.376 \ ft$

Round to hundredth place

$202.38 \ ft$

Final answer

Made in United States
North Haven, CT
08 September 2023

41290781R00180